Archives & Manuscripts

EDITORIAL

Welcome to Volume 51 Number 1, the first issue published for 2023. In 2023, we (Angela Schilling and Dr Jessie Lymn) were appointed as co-General Editors of Archives and Manuscripts by the Australian Society of Archivists Council, and we look forward to further expanding the realms of publishing in the Australian archival context. We thank members this year for their patience as we finalise the Volume 50 print copies and look forward to smoother processes as we continue to embed publishing processes into the journal's production.

This current issue has been Guest Edited by Adrian Cunningham, whose Editorial features on the next pages. The publication of the series of papers delivered at the Documenting Australian Society seminars over the past few years documents the conversations emerging as the archival and wider historical professions engage with the challenges of the project. We encourage further discussion and engagement on the articles and welcome response articles for future issues.

We plan to include one special issue each year and encourage proposals to be submitted to the General Editors (journaleditor@archivists.org.au). We also encourage practitioners and academics to continue to submit their work to the journal and are happy to discuss any potential article ideas with you.

We are also proud to launch a new cover design for the journal. This issue's cover features an image from Jennifer Jerome's reflection piece on the Tasmanian Archives, and we note that future issues will follow suit, highlighting an image from one of the issue's articles.

Angela Schilling
Dr Jessie Lymn

Archives & Manuscripts 2023, 51(1): 10995 - http://dx.doi.org/10.37683/asa.v51.10995

I

GUEST EDITORIAL

Documenting Australian Society Redux

Adrian Cunningham

UNESCO Australian Memory of the World Committee

> The work of archivists is vital for … supporting understandings
> of Australian life through the management and retention
> of its personal, corporate and social memory.
>
> (extract from Australian Society of Archivists,
> 'The Archivist's Mission', 1996)

'The Archivist's Mission' was endorsed by the Council of the Australian Society of Archivists (ASA) in July 1996. From 1999 it was published in the frontispiece of *Archives and Manuscripts* until it disappeared from the journal in 2012 at the time of the switch to Taylor and Francis. Nevertheless, the statement can still be found on the ASA website, so it still constitutes our formal statement of professional intent.[1]

The mission statement confirms our professional commitment to the ambitious cause of documenting Australian society. While the statement implies that this is an endeavour that is a responsibility shared by a range of professional groups, including librarians and museum curators, ASA members understand that archives constitute a vital and perhaps the most important segment of the totality of Australia's documentary heritage. Also implied by the statement is an understanding that, because every archivist and archival program contributes to the cause, Australia's documentary memory is distributed across thousands of keeping places scattered all over the nation. These keeping places range from large national and state institutions through corporate, organisational and collecting archives to small, grassroots, community-led initiatives.

While the mission statement refers to archives as records that have continuing evidential value, this neatly avoids the question – probably the hardest archival question of all – of how do we decide what records have continuing value and what records do not have that value? It is an archival truism that the most important decisions archivists ever make are appraisal decisions. Because records are unique, once a record has been destroyed it is gone forever. Decisions to dispose of records are the ultimate denial of access. Many of us take this solemn responsibility so seriously that it is probably no exaggeration to say that it is one that from time to time keeps us awake at night. Are we getting and keeping the 'right stuff'? Are our holdings truly representative and reflective of the full diversity of society and human experience in Australia? What perspectives are privileged? What and who is being silenced by their omission from our archival estate? Are

*Correspondence: Adrian Cunningham Email: adriancunningham8@gmail.com

the most significant and distinctive aspects of life in Australia adequately documented for the benefit of current and future generations? Who gets to have a say in our appraisal decisions and how defensible, evidence-based, transparent and accountable are those decisions?

Today's archivists have devised sophisticated frameworks and tools to guide their appraisal decision making processes. Our textbook *Keeping Archives* includes an extensive chapter on appraisal. In 2007, the ASA endorsed a formal statement on appraisal, which every ASA member should take the trouble to read carefully.[2] As useful as these things are, their focus is necessarily granular – that is, performing individual appraisal exercises within the context of an archival program's unique mandate and/or collection development policy. Left hanging is the broader and harder question of how does each archival program's appraisal decisions fit into the wider landscape of Australia's national holdings of documentary heritage?

It is that broader question that the 'Documenting Australian Society' initiative seeks to address. Established under the auspices of the UNESCO Australian Memory of the World Program following a national summit meeting in December 2018, the initiative has since run a number of symposia and seminars.[3] The most recent of these was a panel session addressing the question 'How can we rethink our appraisal practices?', held at the 2023 Annual Conference of the ASA in Melbourne.

It is with great pleasure that I was invited to edit this theme issue of *Archives and Manuscripts* devoted to the work of the Documenting Australian Society initiative. Long-term readers of the journal will know that this is not the first time that the journal has devoted a theme issue to the topic of 'Documenting Australian Society'. In 2001, Maggie Shapley edited just such a theme issue. Comparing the content of these two theme issues allows us to contemplate just how much progress has or has not been made on addressing the issue in the ensuing 22 years? Since 2001, we have seen the finalisation of the ASA's 'Statement on Appraisal', referred to above, in addition to the 2018 summit meeting with its grandly titled statement of intent, 'The Canberra Declaration'. At one level, it is fair say that the issue is one that will, by its inherently contestable nature, never be definitively resolved. As such, promoting ongoing debate, discussion and awareness raising may be the most that we can ever hope to achieve. Nevertheless, Summit delegates agreed that we should collectively be working towards something more than just ongoing discussions. My attempt to distil the 'Canberra Declaration' into a succinct set of strategic objectives identified the following five goals:

1. A **National Documentation Strategy** agreed by key industry and professional stakeholders and endorsed by governments.
2. An agreed, evidence-based **framework** (developed through research, dialogue and contestation) for mapping Australia's diverse documentary heritage needs and documentation gaps/silences.
3. Effective **coordination** of collection/acquisition/appraisal planning and activity spanning Australia's entire ecosystem of documentary heritage programs and initiatives.
4. Support for **communities of practice**-based efforts to document aspects of Australian society, especially those of First Nations peoples.
5. Inclusive, active, ongoing **discussion and improved community awareness** of the need to continuously improve the documentation of Australian society for the benefit of current and future generations.

A number of constraints on progress, each of which in their own way provide a justification for the existence of the initiative and its steering committee, can also be identified:

- Funding for documentary heritage preservation will always be limited and must be spent wisely.
- Massive volumes of documentation are created every year in Australia, but only a tiny percentage of the totality can and should be preserved for the use of future generations.
- Deciding what to keep and what not to keep involves making hard decisions.
- The hard decisions made by documentary heritage programs and practitioners are made for the benefit of the Australian community. Therefore, these decisions must be defensible, transparent, consultative, evidence-based and made with reference to the wider body of Australia's distributed holdings of documentary heritage materials.

The articles in this theme issue should be read with all of the foregoing in mind. Most of the articles in this issue are based on presentations made at webinars organised by the Documenting Australian Society initiative. Two articles are from the first of these webinars, which in late 2020 addressed the topic of 'Documenting COVID-19 in Australia. Historian Anthea Hyslop takes the long view of documenting COVID-19, by assessing the state of surviving documentation of the 1919 'Spanish Flu' epidemic. First presented when the COVID pandemic was at its height, this paper provided curators with some fascinating insights into the kinds of contemporaneous documentation that should be prioritised for preservation drawing on the strengths and weaknesses of our documentary holdings of a similar pandemic a century earlier. Digital Humanities scholar Terhi Murmikko-Fuller provides additional intriguing insights and asks some hard questions about capturing documentation of 'ephemeral popular culture', for example social media postings, as enduring evidence of the impact of COVID-19 on Australian society and the lived experience of ordinary Australians.

The second webinar was held in late 2022, addressing the topic 'Honouring the stories of struggle: Reassessing Australian records of disadvantage'. From this webinar, we have two papers. Jennifer Jerome looks at how the lived experience of disadvantage is documented (or not as the case may be) in case files preserved by the Tasmanian State Archives. Jerome argues that case files are, in many respects, the best available evidence of the lived experience of disadvantage, as they are often the most substantial body of documentation of an under-privileged and often silenced segment of society. Despite that, our appraisal regimes for case files often regard this form of record as being of low value and low priority for archival retention. The other piece from the 2022 webinar is a transcript of a video prepared by Robyn Sutherland, CEO of the United Communities welfare service in Adelaide. This video features interviews with the clients of that service where they were invited to reflect on the kinds of documentation these welfare recipients would like to see retained as evidence of their lived experiences. Sutherland reflects that, perhaps inevitably, the records created and retained by her organisation are skewed towards documenting the negative experiences of their clients, rather than creating and capturing a more holistic record of lives of the individuals concerned. This insight raises difficult methodological questions for those of us concerned with the creation and retention of a truly representative body of documentation of Australian society.

The theme issue also includes a highly instructive case study by Jenny Fewster of a nation-wide community of practice that has formed to improve the creation and preservation of documentation of the performing arts in Australia. The collaborative approach to documenting the often ephemeral and evanescent expressions of performance art described by Fewster provides a compelling model for improving the coordination of documentation of other aspects of societal experience. Finally, we have another case study from Louise Curham describing an exercise in participatory appraisal carried out in the context of documenting an individual suburb in the south of Canberra. This article addresses the important issue of how to involve and engage the subjects of appraisal decisions in the processes of determining what documentation should be made and kept of their lives and locales. Too often archivists make appraisal decisions within a 'black box' that privileges their professional expertise over the knowledge and insights of the people about which the documentation is created and for whom the documentation is preserved. Participatory approaches to appraisal are still the exception rather than the norm in our professional practice – a situation that is untenable in an era that claims to value social justice and self-determination.

I am sure that readers will be stimulated by the various articles in this theme issue. I commend them and the goals of the Documenting Australian Society initiative to readers of the journal and look forward to seeing where our evolving discourse on this important topic takes us over the coming years.

Notes

1. Australian Society of Archivists, 'The Archivist's Mission', available at https://www.archivists.org.au/learning-publications/the-archival-profession/archivists-mission, accessed 21 September 2023.
2. Australian Society of Archivists, 'Statement on Appraisal, 2007, available at https://www.archivists.org.au/documents/item/12, accessed 21 September 2023.
3. 'Documenting Australian Society', available at https://amw.org.au/node/111, accessed 21 September 2023.

ARTICLE

Documenting Australian Society: Progress Report on an Initiative of the UNESCO Australian Memory of the World Committee

Adrian Cunningham*

UNESCO Australian Memory of the World Committee

Abstract

The topic of Documenting Australian Society has been something of an occasional perennial on ASA Conference programs since the 1990s. Archives and manuscripts published a theme issue on it in 2001. In December 2018, the UNESCO Australian Memory of the World Program organised a national summit on the topic in Canberra. That summit meeting endorsed 'The Canberra Declaration' as an action agenda for the documentary heritage sectors and agreed that the UNESCO Memory of the World Program should continue to take carriage of the initiative. Since then, a steering committee has been established, and two seminars/webinars have been organised: the first on Documenting COVID-19 in Australia and the second on Documenting the Experiences of Australian on Welfare. This paper discusses the background and objectives of the initiative, its current status and plans for the future.

Keywords: *Documentation strategy*; *Archival silences*; *National coordination*; *Appraisal*; *UNESCO*.

At present in Australia, documentary heritage[1] holdings are built with limited self-awareness of the greater whole. Decisions about what material should be preserved long-term can be reactive and uncoordinated. What are the consequences of this lack of coordination? What picture does the total stock of Australian documentary heritage present? How representative is it in terms of our rich, distinctive and diverse historical experiences, our changing population, localities and multiple national narratives? Are we making the best use of the limited resources that Australia devotes to the cause of preserving and providing access to documentary memory? Australia needs an agreed, transparent and defensible process for making hard decisions about what to make and keep.

A vast quantity of documentation is created and destroyed every year in Australia. With the advent of digital technologies, the world now creates more data every year than it has the physical capacity to store and keep. Only a tiny sliver of this vastness is able to preserve for

*Correspondence: Adrian Cunningham, Email: adriancunningham8@gmail.com

use by future generations. We accept that only a tiny sliver is worth the effort and expense of preserving. But what documentation needs to be included in this sliver? Are there wasteful overlaps and concentrations? Are there gaps and silences? Are we keeping the right stuff? Are there time periods, issues, communities, minorities and phenomena which urgently need targeted documentation strategies? Are there important aspects of life in Australia for which adequate documentation is not created in the first place and which need to be proactively documented before all memory of those activities disappears forever? In short, what documentation does Australia really need to make and keep to enable current and future generations to understand, explain, debate and account for our national collective experiences?

The work of documenting society is carried out by a wide range of organisations, institutions and initiatives that are committed to enabling the long-term preservation of and access to Australia's documentary heritage – or the documentary component of our national estate. To pursue a nationally coordinated approach to our documentation mission, we need to, in the words of David Bearman, 'focus our appraisal methods on selecting what should be documented rather than what documentation should be kept'.[2] In the words of Richard Cox, we need to identify the most 'salient and important features of contemporary institutions and society'[3] and work collectively to ensure that adequate documentary evidence of these features is captured and preserved by archives.

The aim is to achieve better planning and coordination of distributed efforts to preserve and provide access to a representative corpus of documentary heritage materials to help current and future generations understand, debate and interrogate the nature of human experiences in Australia. In an environment of shrinking overall funding for documentary heritage programs, it is more important than ever for practitioners nationwide to be seen to be working together to ensure that we spend our limited budgets in ways that help deliver the best possible collective outcomes for preserving and providing access to a documentary heritage estate.

From time to time, Royal Commissions into significant issues, scandals and injustices in Australian life such as the 'stolen generations', institutional responses to child sexual abuse and forced child migration have highlighted gaps in the available documentation. This in turn has mobilised resources and collaborative action to fill these gaps through initiatives such as oral history and indexing projects. Whilst these efforts have inevitably been somewhat piecemeal, they do show what can be done when there is a collective recognition of the need to do a better job of documenting Australian society.

The question of what aspects of human experience are under-represented or 'silenced' in archival holdings is one that has exercised the minds of archivists for generations. Although it is not a new question, it is one that continues to resonate in our discourse, as is demonstrated by recent attention that has been given to the question of silences in the archive.[4]

What are the diverse and non-mainstream aspects of life in this country that are going under-documented? Where might such documentation be made and kept and by whom? The 'by whom' question is just as critical, if not more critical, than the 'what to keep' question. We should not assume it should just be done by 'us', on 'our' terms. Those groups whose experiences have been neglected, ignored or under-represented in our efforts to date may or may not appreciate being belatedly patronised by established programs and institutions. Our responsibility, I would argue, is not to invite the under-represented into our spaces and establishments – but rather to be willing (and to be seen to be willing) to be invited into the spaces and networks of these other groups to provide some advice, assistance, moral support and resources.

Before delving into the pre-history of the initiative, it is necessary to define its scope. It is primarily focused on decisions regarding what documentary heritage needs to be identified for long-term preservation. Other essential activities such as description of and access to those heritage materials are out of scope. As important as description and access regimes may be, decisions about what to keep and what not to keep are absolutely fundamental to the success or failure of our collective efforts. Decisions (either conscious or unconscious) to not preserve documentation represent the ultimate denial of access to that documentation.

Dealing with the issue in Australia, 1956–2016

Long-time attendees at Australian Society of Archivists (ASA) Conferences will be very aware that the challenge of documenting Australian society has been a topic of professional discussion for many years. In the 1950s, Harold White of the National Library of Australia was arguing to the Paton Inquiry that the main aim of libraries and archives was to build a systematic record of national life and development.[5] This philosophy was echoed by Canadian Dominion Archivist W. Kaye Lamb in 1973 when he visited Australia to investigate and report on future directions for the then Commonwealth Archives Office. The vision of there being a coordinated national archival system resembled the holistic 'total archives' philosophy that prevailed (and still prevails) in Canada and was enshrined in Australian law with the passage of the *Archives Act* in 1983. Sadly, a combination of under-resourcing and passive opposition to the idea has meant that those provisions of the *Archives Act* have rarely been a priority for the National Archives of Australia, which has usually defined its role as beginning and ending with Commonwealth records. Documentation initiatives were left to others such as the Business Archives Council, the Australian Science Archives Project, the Australian Women's Archives Project and the National Library's Register of Australian Archives and Manuscripts (RAAM). Each of these separate initiatives was highly commendable in their own right but was left to live or die based on the heroic efforts of particular groups and individuals, being isolated initiatives pursued in the absence of any national system of support or mechanism for agreeing and addressing gaps and priorities.

The phrase 'documentation strategy' entered the archival lexicon courtesy of Helen Samuels, who wrote about it in an article called 'Who Controls the Past?' in *The American Archivist* in 1986. Samuels defined a documentation strategy as 'a plan formulated to assure the documentation of an ongoing issue, activity, or geographic area (e.g. the operation of the government of the state of New York, labor unions in the United States, the impact of technology on the environment)'.[6] In Australia, the possibility of implementing a nationally coordinated documentation strategy was aired in 1992 at the cross-disciplinary national summit 'Towards Federation 2001', convened by Deputy National Librarian, Eric Wainwright. Another National Library staffer, Manuscript Librarian Graeme Powell, took up the challenge in an article in *Archives and Manuscripts* in 1996. Powell surveyed the state of our documentary estate, as recorded in the then *Guide to Collections of Manuscripts*, which had been collated and published for many years by the National Library. He found a preponderance of personal papers of creative writers, academics, pastoralists and businessmen. Correspondingly, he found many notable absences. Notwithstanding the trade union holdings of the Noel Butlin Archives and University of Melbourne Archives, where were the papers of shearers, waterside workers, nurses, factory workers, Aboriginal activists, housewives and European immigrants?[7]

In 1997, I gave a paper at the ASA's annual conference titled 'From Here to Eternity: Collecting Archives and the Need for National Documentation Strategy'.[8] In 1999, Michael Piggott took up the cause in a paper delivered to the National Scholarly Communications Forum Round Table on Archives in the National Research Infrastructure titled 'A National Approach to Archival Appraisal and Collecting'. In turn, Piggott's paper inspired Maggie Shapley in 2001 to edit a theme issue of *Archives and Manuscripts* focused on the issue of documenting Australian Society. This issue included articles by Kirsten Thorpe on Indigenous records; Sigrid McCausland on documenting protest movements; Don Boadle on documenting rural and regional Australia; Marie-Louise Ayres on 20th Century literary archives; and Richard

Cashman on sports archives. In the same year, Sue McKemmish wrote that there was 'no coherent, collaborative, nationally coordinated, encompassing fourth dimension collection policy framework for the whole of Australian society'.[9]

After that, the issue faded into the background of our discourse until Michael Piggott again picked up the cudgel in his valedictory keynote address on the absence of an Australian archival system to the 2008 ASA annual conference in Perth. In this paper, Piggott proposed four rules for any such system:

1. Be inclusive
2. Form the machinery
3. Develop a documentation plan
4. Know what you stand for.[10]

Once again, the issue slow burned for a few years, is re-emerging as a hot topic for discussion at three successive ASA annual conferences between 2013 and 2015, and led particularly by Sigrid McCausland, Kim Eberhard, Colleen McEwen and Maggie Shapley. In the midst of that, I once again weighed into the fray with an article in *Archives and Manuscripts* that revisited my 1997 ASA Conference paper.[11] All of this chatter was very interesting, but it did not really lead anywhere. There seemed to be consensus that a national documentation strategy would be a nice thing to have, but no one was able to advance the idea in any concrete manner. Sigrid McCausland was plotting with Michael Piggott at Tilley's wine bar in Lyneham, Canberra, about how to get things moving. At the time, I was a near neighbour of Sigrid's – both of us living in the Brisbane suburb of Annerley. When she was diagnosed with her terminal illness in 2016, we had some intense discussions about how to make sure the idea got some real legs. I made a deathbed promise to her that it would not die with her, and that I would do all I could to get something happening. I moved back to Canberra and resumed the plotting with Michael Piggott at Tilley's wine bar. Mindful of his second rule from his valedictory keynote, we agreed that the only current avenue for forming some machinery was the UNESCO Australian Memory of the World Program. With its national, pan-disciplinary focus on preserving documentary heritage, Memory of the World was the nearest equivalent to the long defunct Collections Council of Australia as a possible suitable sponsor for an initiative to progress efforts at documenting Australian society. We approached the Memory of the World Committee proposing a national summit to explore whether key stakeholders were genuinely interested in the idea or not. The Committee agreed enthusiastically to our proposal, and so we set about planning a summit gathering in Canberra in December 2018. David Fricker, of the National Archives of Australia, generously agreed to sponsor the event.

The 2018 Summit and 'Canberra Declaration'
The invitation-only Summit featured two invited overseas speakers – Laura Millar from Canada and Mark Crookston from New Zealand – the aim being to let delegates hear about similar efforts in two other societies with similar histories of indigenous first nations and British/multicultural settler societies. A range of local speakers including archivists, librarians, curators, historians and social commentators filled out the program.

The aim of the event was to test the appetite of key players for pursuing a more coordinated approach to building a distributed Australian documentary heritage estate that is as representative as possible of the full diversity and complexity of life in Australia. We were quite prepared for the possibility that the answer to our question might be, 'no thanks – not that interested' or perhaps 'nice idea, but it is unrealistic and we have better things to do with our limited resources'. If so, we would have walked away telling ourselves, 'well, we had to try – but now we know the idea won't fly'.

But that did not happen. In fact, the summit delegates endorsed the idea and passed a 'Canberra Declaration' committing themselves and/or their organisations to work collaboratively to pursue a representative national estate of documentary heritage. The first five points of the declaration are all motherhood statements. They summarise the issue and explain why it matters. The remaining points are all action items. These points can be summarised as follows:

1. Identify key issues, communities, groups and partners to involve in further discussions
2. Pursue collaborative research into strengths, gaps and weaknesses of existing national holdings + models and strategies for improving those holdings
3. Engage with governments about policies and funding for improved planning and coordination
4. The NAA (National Archives of Australia); NLA (National Library of Australia); NFSA (National Film and Sound Archive) and AIATSIS (Australian Institute of Aboriginal and Torres Strait Islander Studies) to pursue joint and inclusive leadership for a national system for documentary heritage preservation
5. Develop a collaborative plan of action.

Progress since the Summit
Since the Summit, a small group of summit organisers and delegates, together with some Memory of the World Committee members and others, have been active in discussing the initiative with range of interested organisations and academic researchers. Initially, we decided that our most pressing need was to initiate some rigorous research to give us a more informed understanding of the current state of documentary heritage preservation in Australia. This research could explore potential evidence sources and frameworks for identifying gaps in holdings and ways of prioritising the documentation of important but neglected or under-represented aspects of life in Australia. We felt that we needed a solid evidence base to inform the planning and coordination of efforts and that research (in addition to inclusive community participation and consultation) is needed to build and test this evidence base.

We have had many useful and detailed discussions with a wide variety of academics across Australia from a variety of subject disciplines. All expressed interest in and support for the initiative, and many very good ideas and suggestions have been forthcoming. These discussions are continuing but are yet to bear fruit in any viable research funding proposal to the Australian Research Council.

At the suggestion of Memory of the World Committee member Rachel Watson, we agreed to broaden the focus of the Documenting Australian Society Initiative to place more emphasis on fostering grassroots, community-led documentation efforts. Rachel proposed a self-selecting 'communities of practice' model – a 'bottom up' approach to documenting society that could complement and enrich the more 'top down', planned and coordinated approaches pursued by peak bodies and national documentation frameworks. An excellent example of such a community of practice is one coordinated by AusStage that is documenting the performing arts in Australia. This is a great model for other potential engagements with grassroots practitioners, including Community Heritage Grants recipients.

In 2020, we established a steering committee to guide the initiative into the future and which will report to the UNESCO Australian Memory of the World Committee. The steering committee, whose initial focus is on pursuing the action items from the Canberra Declaration, consists of members of the parent Committee, in addition to representatives from the Australian Society of Archivists (position currently vacant following the departure of Leisa Gibbons), Kirsten Thorpe (representing Indigenous perspectives) and key national collecting institutions named in the Canberra Declaration. In future, we hope to broaden the membership of the steering committee by including representatives from GLAM Peak, the Australian Library and Information Association, NSLA (National and State Libraries Australia) and individuals who can represent grassroots community heritage practitioners and users.

Also in 2020, with the support of the National Archives, we organised a webinar on the highly topical issue of Documenting COVID-19 in Australia. This event featured: Commonwealth Chief Health Officer Dr Brendan Murphy; pandemic historian Anthea Hyslop; freelance curator Lauren Carroll Harris; Scott Stephens from the ABC; Jaye Weatherburn from the Digital Preservation Coalition; digital humanities and media academics from ANU and the Queensland University of Technology; and speakers from different national collecting institutions. A video of this event can be viewed on YouTube.

In 2022, we commenced a strategic planning process facilitated by Shane Breynard. One outcome of that process has been agreement on Vision and Mission statements:

Vision
Nationwide holdings of documentary heritage that are inclusive and representative of the wide diversity of Australian experience and endeavours, past and present.

Mission
To enable this vision, we will foster an ecosystem of research, planning and coordination that supports documentary heritage programs, practitioners and communities of practice, and that engages broadly across Australian society.

In late 2022, we are organised another webinar/seminar over the road at the National Archives of Australia, that is co-sponsored by the ASA and the National Archives. This free event has the title 'Honouring the stories of struggle: Reassessing Australian records of disadvantage'. The event will have two sessions: one asking the question 'What evidence should be preserved?' and the other asking the question 'What evidence is being preserved?'. The first session will feature care leaver Dr Frank Golding; Robyn Sutherland from Uniting Communities; genealogist Danielle Lautrec and UTS social policy academics Eva Cox and Professor Nareen Young – the latter speaking on Indigenous perspectives. The second session will feature speakers from the National Archives of Australia, National Library of New Zealand and Jenny Jerome from Tasmania, in addition to Cassie Findlay talking about privacy issues.

Other models
Australia is not the only country that has the challenge of selecting and preserving a representative body of documentary heritage as a systematic and inclusive record of national life and experiences. I have already mentioned Canada and New Zealand as sources of inspiration for our efforts. New Zealand is a particular inspiration for our work. There is, in New Zealand, explicit acknowledgement that they have a thing called a 'national documentary heritage system'. Their National Library, Archives New Zealand, Te Papa and their film and sound archive work together to exercise leadership and provide support for this system and its associated 'Preserving the Nation's Memory' work program, called Tahuhu. Senior positions have been created in these institutions with responsibility for the liaison, coordination and strategic relationship management that the program includes. The relevant Minister requires all budget bids to demonstrate how they impact on and relate to the documentary heritage system. As an example of this system at work, there is the 'We are the Beneficiaries' project led out of the National Library of New Zealand. This project is run on the principles of co-design involving representatives of the welfare beneficiary groups and individuals in New Zealand whose

stories and experiences the project aims to document. I am delighted that Jessica Moran from New Zealand will be speaking about this project at our seminar on Friday.

In the United States, there is a brilliant initiative called 'Documenting the Now'. This project is funded by the Mellon Foundation and Princeton University Library and governed by the Shift Collective, which aims to achieve 'equity by design'. It develops open-source tools and community-centred practices that support the ethical collection and use and preservation of publicly available content shared on web and social media. Documenting the Now responds to the public's use of social media for chronicling historically significant events as well as demand from scholars, students, archivists and others, seeking a user-friendly means of collecting and preserving this type of digital content.[12]

Future steps?

The Documenting Australian Society steering committee will continue reaching out to new partners and stakeholder in an effort to broaden our reach and sustain our efforts. We will keep a close watch on similar initiatives in other countries and will seek to emulate good models and initiatives. With the new Government in Canberra developing a new national cultural policy, we hope that there will be a space in this policy for the kind of coordination of efforts and outcomes that is our vision for documentary heritage in Australia. Funding for the initiative is an ongoing challenge, given that the UNESCO Australian Memory of the World Program has no reliable source of income. We are most grateful, therefore, for the sponsorship of the ASA and the National Archives for events such as Friday's seminar – for otherwise, there would be very little that we could accomplish.

We will never achieve a state of perfection – or documentary heritage nirvana – regardless of how well we cooperate and regardless of how clear and compelling our vision might be. We will always have gaps and inconsistencies, not the least because of the inevitability of funding shortfalls, political complexities and the irreconcilability of contestable and contingent perspectives and world views across our domains. Indeed, it is the nature of this complex and contingent beast that I think we will and should always be constructively dissatisfied with the results of our collective efforts. Continuous improvement will always be necessary.

But just because we might never achieve perfection does not mean we are not all obliged morally and professionally to work together as well as we can to do the best job we possibly can do given all of the constraints and realities mentioned earlier. It would be unfair for future generations to condemn us for trying but failing to achieve perfection. But future generations would be absolutely entitled to condemn us if we don't even try to do something about the challenge or, worse, pretend that the problem does not exist.

Collectively, there is a need to develop and operationalise frameworks and mechanisms that can help guide the making of hard choices and agreeing and allocating responsibilities. These frameworks and mechanisms need to be evidence-based, defensible, coherent, realistic, inclusive, holistic, contestable, transparent and capable of evolving. The work needs to be informed by a thorough understanding of the current state of Australian documentary heritage holdings – its strengths, weaknesses, gaps and overlaps. Our baseline, if you like. More importantly, and more far more challenging, it needs to be informed by knowledge of and some level of agreement on what is important and distinctive about the diversity and complexity of life in Australia that has to be reflected in our documentary heritage in order to help current and future generations interrogate and understand Australian society. Our responsibility is to ensure that important aspects of Australian life are not neglected as a result of well-meaning but disjointed, fragmented and ad hoc efforts pursued in the absence of a holistic regime that provides support and resources to diverse, community-driven documentary preservation programs.

The objectives of the initiative are ambitious, if not audacious. It will not be easy to make progress. We must avoid the temptation to try to 'boil the ocean' but rather make progress in small and incremental steps. But if something is important, the fact that it may be difficult is no reason not to attempt to advance the issue, and that we would stand to be condemned if we do not try our best to achieve success. Gallant failure is preferable to a lack of action, or indeed a lack of acknowledgement of the importance of the issue.

Notes

1. For the purposes of this article, the author uses the definition of 'documentary heritage' that has been adopted by the UNESCO Memory of the World Programme. See UNESCO, General Guidelines of the Memory of the World (MoW) Programme, Paris, 2021, p. 2, available at: https://unesdoc.unesco.org/ark:/48223/pf0000378405?posInSet=25&queryId=f3fa4032-9934-4376-a95b-720fae659c27 accessed 23 September 2023.
2. David Bearman, Archival Methods, Archives and Museums Informatics, Pittsburgh, 1989, pp. 14–15.
3. Richard Cox, 'The Documentation Strategy and Archival Appraisal Principles: A Different Perspective', *Archivaria*, vol. 38, 1994, p. 24.
4. Michael Moss and David Thomas (eds.), Archival Silences: Missing, Lost and Uncreated Archives, Routledge, London, 2021; Kieran Hegarty, 'Representing Biases, Inequalities and Silences in National Web Archives: Social, Material and Technical Dimensions', *Archives and Manuscripts*, vol. 50, no. 1, September 2022, pp. 31–46.
5. Michael Piggott, '"An Important and Delicate Assignment": The Paton Inquiry, 1956–57', *Australian Academic and Research Libraries*, vol. 21, no. 4, 1990, pp. 213–223.
6. Helen Willa Samuels, 'Who Controls the Past?', *The American Archivist*, vo. 49, no. 2, 1986, pp. 109–124.
7. Graeme Powell, 'The Collecting of Personal and Private Papers in Australia', *Archives and Manuscripts*, vol. 24, no. 1, May 1996, pp. 62–77.
8. Adrian Cunningham, 'From Here to Eternity: Collecting Archives and the Need for a National Documentation Strategy', *Lasie*, vol. 29, no. 1, March 1998, pp. 32–45.
9. Sue McKemmish, 'Placing Records Continuum Theory and Practice', *Archival Science* 1, 2001, p. 351.
10. Michael Piggott, 'The Australian Archival System, 1971-2008: A Valedictory Appraisal', *Archives and Manuscripts*, vol. 36, no. 2, November 2008, pp. 189–207.
11. Adrian Cunningham, 'Eternity Revisited: In Pursuit of a National Documentation Strategy and a National Archival System', *Archives and Manuscripts*, vol. 42, no. 2, July 2014, pp. 165–170.
12. See: http://www.docnow.io/

REFLECTION ARTICLE

Documenting the Lived Experience of Disadvantage in Tasmania

Jennifer Jerome*

Abstract

This article discusses how government and community records in the Tasmanian Archives provide evidence of how well Tasmanians have met their need for safe shelter. It provides a brief overview of the structures that have guided the development of the Tasmanian Archives collection – how decisions have been made regarding what to add, or exclude, from the collection. It also investigates if records of housing and housing access have been prioritised for long-term retention, and if not, why? The role of case files as key records of lived experience is discussed, with the aim of sparking discourse on the strengths and weaknesses of archival collections as they record disadvantage and the lived experience of Australians. This article is based upon a presentation given by the author at the 2022 Australian Memory of the World Documenting Australian Society Seminar in Canberra.

Keywords: *Disadvantage*; *case files*; *housing*; *records retention*.

ase files are the most voluminous and routine documents produced by modern bureaucracies. In governments, business, universities and similar corporate bodies, they fill records offices and records centres to the brim. If acquired, they threaten to overwhelm archives everywhere with mountains of paper. Their electronic counter parts, whilst less bulky, also present complex problems. Yet, with this avalanche of information are many gems, which enrich our understanding of the past. Indeed, such gems can be a sparkling reflection of citizens' voice, individually and collectively, and sometimes, they are the only such reflection that survives for posterity. Without the patterns and themes uncovered by research in such records, the history of institutions could be told, but not that of people. Terry Cook, 1991[1]

Shelter is an intrinsic human need.[2] Not being able to access adequate shelter is a clear sign of disadvantage. In looking at records of disadvantage and struggle, we can use both government and community records to find evidence of how well or otherwise Australians have met their need for safe shelter. Our national, state and local archives are arguably the best places to access these records, but what records do they hold? Have records of housing and housing access been prioritised for long-term retention? In this

---

*Correspondence: Jennifer Jerome, Email: jennifer.jerome@libraries.tas.gov.au

paper I will investigate this topic from the perspective of the Tasmanian Archives and its collections. I will give a brief overview of the structures that have guided how the collection of the Tasmanian Archives has developed – how decisions have been made on what to add, or exclude, from the collection. I will give examples of records in the Archives, records that have been included thorough both proactive and passive acquisition practices. Through this, I hope to spark a conversation around the strengths and weaknesses of the Tasmanian archival collection as it records disadvantage and the lived experience of Tasmanians.

Developing the Tasmanian Archives

The Tasmanian Archives aims to be the repository of the documented heritage of the state of Tasmania. Its collection includes archival material from both the State Government and the community. The Archives aims to preserve the core records of the state[3] and evidence of the functions of Government. If they are to fulfil this aim, the Tasmanian Archives should include a wide range of documentation around where Tasmanians live, the kinds of housing they live in and struggles around accessing and retaining housing.

The Tasmanian Archives and the State Library both come under the banner of Libraries Tasmania. This unique situation allows clients to access both archival and state library items from the one service. The authority to develop and preserve a state archive comes from the Archives Act 1983 (Tas)[4] and the Libraries Act 1984 (Tas).[5] Whilst these

Figure 1. Hobart – Wapping, c.1900, Tasmanian Archives: PH30/1/4967.

Archives & Manuscripts 2023, 51 (1): 10953 - http://dx.doi.org/10.37683/asa.v51.10953

pieces of legislation establish Libraries Tasmania's role, neither Act prescribes in detail what the organisation should define as appropriate or significant documentary heritage. This allows a great amount of flexibility when determining what will become part of the collection.

The Tasmanian Archives is accessed by a diverse range of people – both in person and online. Many researchers are hoping to find facts and figures; others are looking for more in-depth or detailed information, something to give context and depth to basic data. One of the most common reasons that people access the archives is for genealogical purposes. At Libraries Tasmania, staff create in-depth descriptions of records to explain why they were created and what they include. They also provide research assistance to guide clients to places, both archival and published, that might hold the information they are looking for.

As a general policy, Tasmanian Government records are selected to be State Archives when they show the decision-making processes of government and the implementation and outcome of those decisions. Staff appraise the records of a Government Agency aiming to retain records that show:

- the authority and structure of Government
- the best evidence of Government functions and programs
- evidence of the Government's influence and effect on communities and individual lives, and
- environmental management and change in Tasmania.

In addition, there is a commitment to retaining records that can be utilised to check on and enforce government accountability, and which allow Tasmanians to find the evidence they need to ensure their rights and entitlements are afforded.

Along with Government records, the Tasmanian Archives collects and preserves community archives. The Community Archive collection is comprised of personal, family, organisational and corporate records. Staff select for inclusion records that:

- provide evidence of Tasmania and its people,
- record significant events in Tasmania,
- reflect the day-to-day lives of Tasmanians over time, and
- include the political, social, cultural, religious, economic, and natural history of Tasmania.

Proactive donations are heavily relied upon to grow the community archives. Over the last four years, an average of 80 new donations of community archives have been accepted per year. Resourcing has seen Tasmanian Archives favour not favours a passive collecting approach. It is only in exceptional situations that the Archives is able to choose what it wants to collect and then proactively go and approach possible donors.

Records of housing and access to housing within the archives
The Tasmanian Archives and Tasmanian State Library collections include many records of houses and development – for example house plans, building applications and family histories that detail land settlement and property development.

If a person did not own a property but rented a place to live or lived with their employer, then this is reflected in census records, post office directories and electoral rolls, as well as in assessment and valuation rolls. The Archives also include records of public housing and the

Figure 2. L: Plan – Public House, Tasmanian Archives: PWD266/1/89.

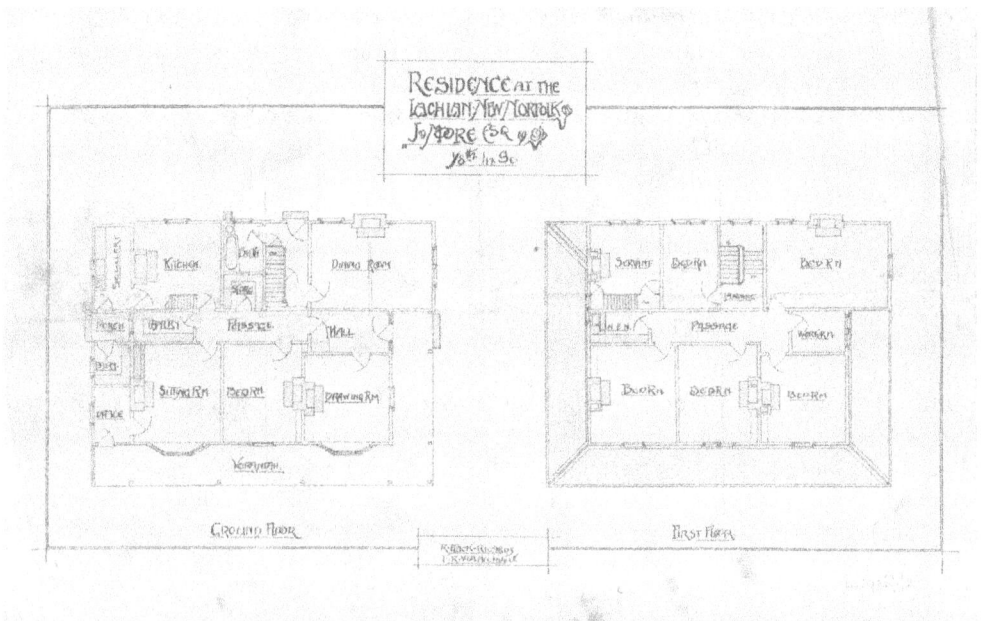

Figure 3. R: Plan – Residence at Lachlan, New Norfolk for J Moore Esq Architect R Flack-Ricards – Ground and first floor plan, Tasmanian Archives: NS2936/1/2.

development of subdivisions. More broadly, the Archives has records that contain information on the financial context of housing affordability in Tasmania. These records include many 'facts and figures'.

Archives & Manuscripts 2023, 51(1): 10953 - http://dx.doi.org/10.37683/asa.v51.10953

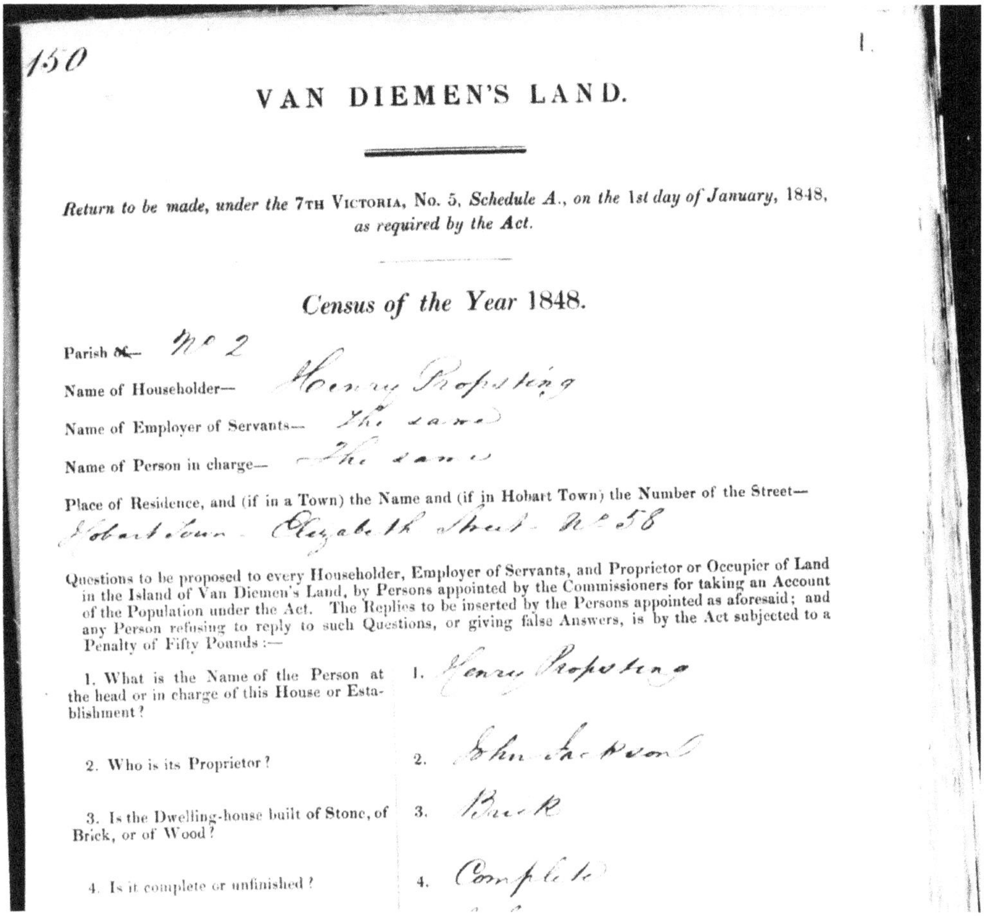

150

1.

VAN DIEMEN'S LAND.

Return to be made, under the 7TH VICTORIA, No. 5, *Schedule A., on the 1st day of January*, 1848, *as required by the Act.*

Census of the Year 1848.

Parish No 2

Name of Householder— Henry Propsting

Name of Employer of Servants— The same

Name of Person in charge— The same

Place of Residence, and (if in a Town) the Name and (if in Hobart Town) the Number of the Street—

Hobart Town Elizabeth Street No 58

Questions to be proposed to every Householder, Employer of Servants, and Proprietor or Occupier of Land in the Island of Van Diemen's Land, by Persons appointed by the Commissioners for taking an Account of the Population under the Act. The Replies to be inserted by the Persons appointed as aforesaid; and any Person refusing to reply to such Questions, or giving false Answers, is by the Act subjected to a Penalty of Fifty Pounds:—

1. What is the Name of the Person at the head or in charge of this House or Establishment? — 1. Henry Propsting

2. Who is its Proprietor? — 2. John Jackson

3. Is the Dwelling-house built of Stone, of Brick, or of Wood? — 3. Brick

4. Is it complete or unfinished? — 4. Complete

Figure 4. HOBART Parish 2 Return 150-299 (Census1848), Tasmanian Archives: CEN1/1/80.

For the period prior to the establishment of the Tasmanian Housing Division in 1908, Tasmanian Government records related to housing can found within three broad areas:

- Records recording the regulation and development of land for settlement and agriculture
- Records recording management of and reporting on issues that come from dense infrastructure such as drainage and environmental pests
- and records recording overseeing a range of charitable institutions, residential facilities, hospitals and schools.

Examples of these records include House of Assembly Papers,[6] annual reports of Institutions, correspondence of the Colonial Secretaries Office,[7] records of entities such as the Charitable Grants Department[8] and Local Government records. Council minutes can also include records of housing disputes and evidence of petitions for housing assistance from individual residents or charitable organisations. For example, Tasmanian Archives holds the records of the Hobart City Council, which include (very sparse) minutes of the 'Houses for the Poor Committee' set up by the Council in 1904 to address poverty and housing-related issues.[9]

Since 1908, there have been quite a few departments with housing as their core responsibility (see Table 1). Each of these government agencies or departments is required by the Archives Act, and sometimes under their own establishing legislation, to send permanent records to Archives.

The process of negotiating which Government records become State Archives is complex. The Tasmanian Archives works continually with Government Agencies to assist with records disposal. Together documents called schedules or authorities are developed that outline which of an Agency's records need to be kept permanently, and those that can be retained for temporary periods of varied length. Generally, Government records that are set for permanent retention in disposal schedules include documents that give broad overviews of the programs and activities undertaken by an Agency. Key types of records usually made permanent include policy documents, statistical reporting, significant administrative correspondence, meeting agendas and minutes and records of compliance with standards. For records related to clients and customers of services, or of the staff that run a service, only registers or lists tend to be classified as permanent. In-depth files, sometimes called 'case files', are often classified as 'temporary'. This is usually because their extent is thought to be too large, and their contents thought to be too repetitive or mundane, to be of high long-term value.[10,11]

'Temporary' records are set for destruction in the future. This may be anywhere from a few years to over a 100 years. Temporary records may be saved from destruction by chance and accident or through a reassessment of their value. For example, if a Royal Commission or industrial issue occurs, the information in a previously 'temporary' record may be reassessed as having a higher value. In these cases, a disposal freeze can be put in place where record destruction is halted until the freeze is removed.[12]

Researchers approaching Government archives need to be aware that, because of decisions around disposal authorisation, many housing-related case files – that is, files that comprehensively document a family, individual or property – tend not to be found in the archives. This can be seen, for example, in disposal schedule DS22, which was issued by the Tasmanian State Archives in 1995.[13] DS22 authorised retention or destruction of records of the Housing Services Program for the Department of Community and Health Services. DS22 designated many case files or files of the day-to-day management of housing as temporary. For example, 'house history files', which include the condition of public housing and records of the management of tenancies, are both temporary.

Table 1. Tasmanian Departments with a core responsibility for the housing function

1908–1984:	Housing Division (within Agricultural Bank of Tasmania) (TA53)
1951–1957:	Office of the Minister for Housing (TA985)
1953–1977:	Housing Department (1) (TA68)
1976–1980:	Office of the Minister for Housing and Construction (TA741)
1977–1983:	Department of Housing and Construction (TA879)
1984–1989:	Housing Department (2) (TA880)
1989–1993:	Department of Community Services (TA769)
1993–2016:	Housing Tasmania (within Dept of Communities) (TA1593)
1993 –	Aboriginal Housing Service Tasmania (associated with Housing Tasmania) (TA1712)
2009 –	Rental Services (TA2142)
2016–2022:	Housing, Disability and Community Services (TA2177)
2022–	Homes Tasmania (TA2229)

Case files and personal stories

Case files, or records that provide information on particular people or places, can be fantastic sources for information on how a government service actually operated in practice. However, these files can be numerous depending on the number of clients that a service has. Large runs of records take up repository space and can be highly repetitive in content. When case files do exist in the Tasmanian Archives, they are often not in full runs. This is the result of re-evaluations in the 1980s and 90s of records transferred earlier to the Archives. In some cases, whole sets of records were destroyed; in others, a sample was retained. These samples were either randomly chosen or selected for their significance or size. An example is the series 'Applications for Assistance and associated Correspondence under the *Housing Department Act* 1938 and 1946 (Srd)'.[14] The records in this series relate to a government-guaranteed advance scheme that allowed people to, without a deposit, apply for housing loans. Just a sample of this series – one box with 16 files – remains.

For researchers looking to find personal housing stories, the records of the Fair Rent Boards[15] can be more useful. Established in the late 1930s, Fair Rent Boards assessed applications from renters and landlords regarding disputes over rents. Records in the Tasmanian Archives include both applications for evictions and determinations of the Board. A set of Fair Rent Board records[16] in the Tasmanian Archives includes applications for rent determinations and reductions. These applications give a window into housing conditions of the time. For example, in many cases, landlords are recorded as seeking to raise rents, yet inspections included in the records show that properties needed repair or in fact were not suitable for habitation.

Other useful housing-related case file records (that have not been sampled) include those from Federal and then State Government Schemes put in place to grow the housing stock in Tasmania, or other programs such as the Solider Settlement Scheme. For example, there are 3119 files for clients who received housing loans from the Agricultural Bank or the Tasmanian Development Authority.[17]

A look within a case file

The Tasmanian Archives includes a set of housing-related case files – the series called 'Yellow Back Files for Premises purchased or vacated'.[18] Created by the Housing Department, this series once documented all of public housing that had been purchased or vacated by tenants. In 2023, all that remains of the series is a small sample – just seven boxes – including material from 1947 to 1977. Included within these boxes is a 1960s case file for the Flynn family.

The Flynns are described as living in one room at Carlton Street in the Hobart suburb of New Town. Mr Flynn is listed as being an employed Milkman, with Mrs Flynn listed as looking after their 16-month-old son and expecting another child. The file contains information about the Flynn's urgent need to be assigned a property by the Housing Department. There is also a letter from a doctor, recommending that Mrs Flynn needs better accommodation, letters from two local politicians, and an inspection that the Department undertook so that they could confirm that the family did, indeed, need new accommodation. The file follows the Flynn's increasingly desperate pleas. By September 1960, their power had been turned off at their New Town accommodation. One month later, the Flynns had signed a contract to purchase a Tecoma Road Risdon Vale property. Risdon Vale was a housing subdivision area established by the Government. The file includes papers showing the family falling into arrears in payments and closes in 1964 with the family's purchase contract terminated due to 'health reasons' of Mr Flynn and his children.

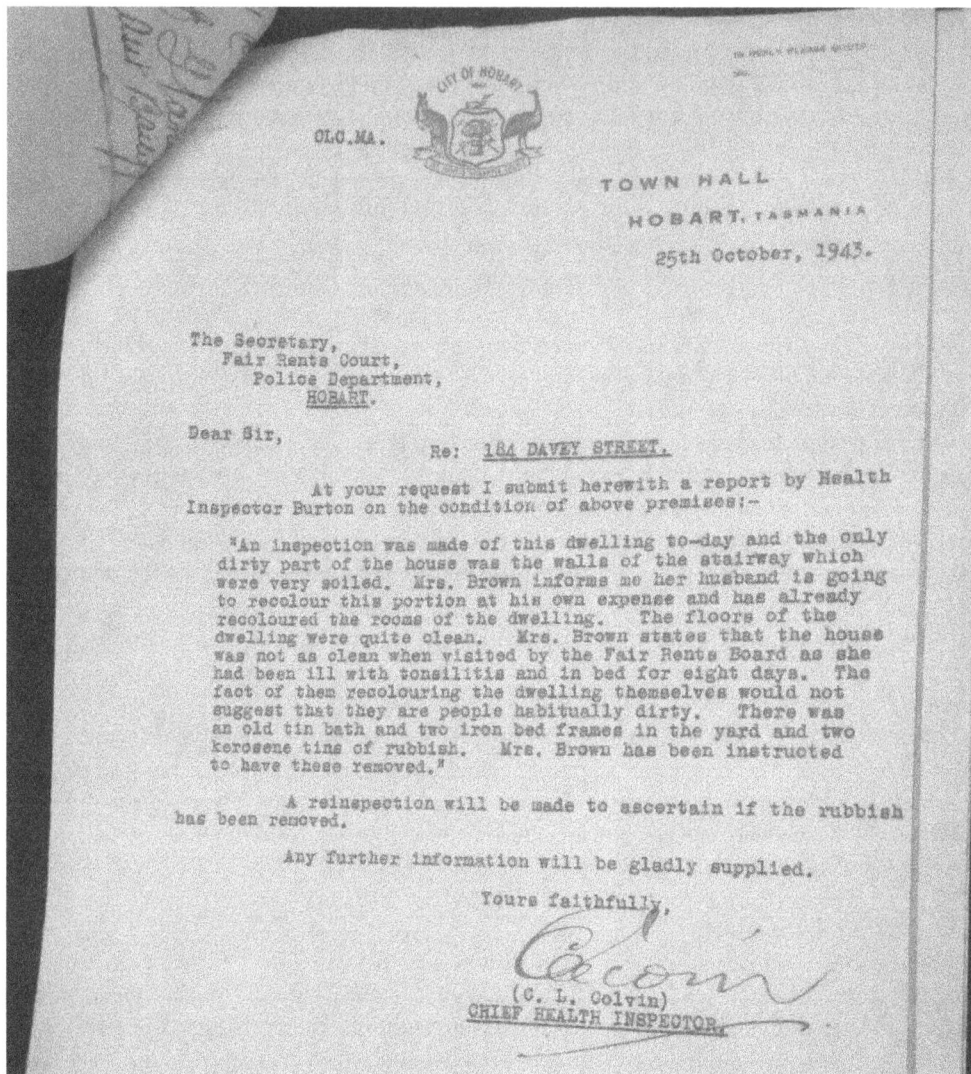

Figure 5. Sample page, Applications Nos. 301-400 for Rent Determinations and Reductions, with Inspection Reports and Associated Papers. Tasmanian Archives: AGD41/1/1.

'Housing' in the community (non-government) archives

A range of Community Archives balances out the Tasmanian Archives collection of Tasmanian records related to housing. Some of the earliest community records related to assisting people with housing can be found in the records of Church organisations and Tasmanian Benevolent Societies. The first Benevolent Society to be established was in Hobart in 1859,[19] followed by Launceston[20] in 1869 and Burnie in 1908.[21]

The records of the Hobart Benevolent Society are all in one series.[22] This series includes minutes, assistance registers (with the basic details of people assisted) and annual reports. Sadly, the individual case files of those assisted have not been kept. The Society minutes from 1933 make a note that they were destroyed:

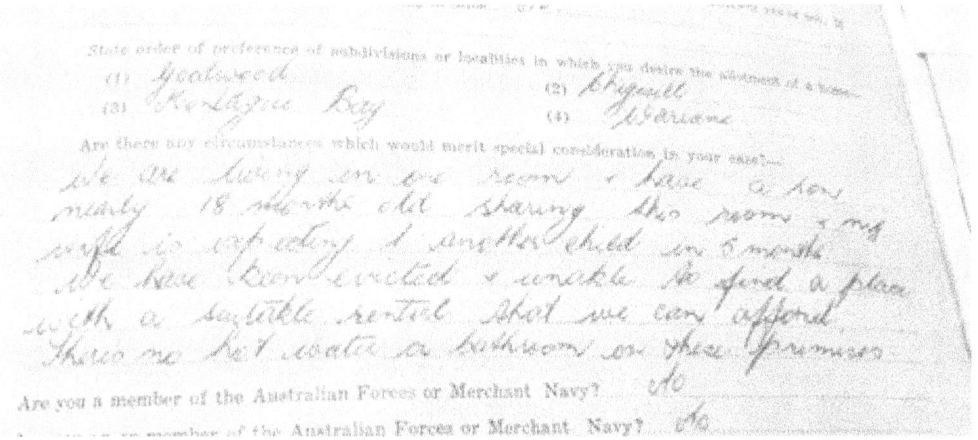
State order of preference of subdivisions or localities in which you desire the allotment of a house

(1) Goodwood (2) Chigwell

(3) Montague Bay (4) Warrane

Are there any circumstances which would merit special consideration in your case?—

We are living in one room & have a son nearly 18 months old sharing this room & my wife is expecting another child in 5 months. We have been evicted & unable to find a place with a suitable rental that we can afford. There is no hot water or bathroom on these premises

Are you a member of the Australian Forces or Merchant Navy? No

Are you a member of the Australian Forces or Merchant Navy? No

Figure 6. Example record, Yellow Back Files for Premises purchased or vacated, Tasmanian Archives: HD9/1/1.

> The Secretary drew attention to the accumulation of the details of cases which were many seven years old and of little value as the names of persons concerned were recorded in the minutes – resolved that the detailed records would not be kept longer than 10 years.

Instead, researchers can get a general feel from the records of Hobart Benevolent Society of the state of housing distress in Hobart: For example, a statement from 1933 includes:

> …. (this resolution) expresses its conviction that the present system of State Relief is distressingly inadequate …. The unemployed have had to subsist for a long period upon allowances barely sufficient to keep themselves and their families alive. They have no surplus over and above the amount required to obtain food, and they have been unable to pay landlords, Doctors, Dentists and others, or to buy necessary clothing …[23]

The only record that the Tasmanian Archives has for the Launceston Benevolent Society is one report book of an Inspector.[24] This example from this book shows the situation in the 1870s of a Mrs Huskinson and her five children. Mrs Huskinson's voice is not heard, instead we have the assessment of the inspector:

> Mrs Huskinson (668) a widow with 5 children residing in …, has been relieved since Oct 18th 1864, I heard Mrs H was misconducting herself and I went to her and told her if there was a repetition of her conduct the Society would stop her rations

> ….Mrs H was misconducting herself and also keeping a brothel….. I informed her that the committee would surely discontinue her rations unless she led a different life. She has three girls at home quite old enough to see and know what is going on in the house, and also in the neighbourhood which is infested with prostitutes and men of the lowest characters….

Also prominent in Tasmania was the Hobart City Mission, established in Hobart in 1852. Records held at the Tasmanian Archives for the Mission include meeting minutes.[25] The minutes include information about donations collected, visits made, and outreach and reflect various concerns at different times – for example religious outreach, working on temperance matters and assisting with poverty. Another important non-Government group that arose in the 1940s was the 'Slum Abolition League' 1940-1945,[26] and Tasmanian Archives has a small set of correspondence and associated papers of the League. Church records can be a very useful source of information on the living conditions of Tasmanians. Churches are good record keepers, and many have now deposited their records with the Tasmanian Archives. The Tasmanian Archives has records from a wide range of religious organisations,[27] including the Anglican Church, the Methodist Churches, the Presbyterian Churches, the Uniting Church, the Hobart Hebrew Congregation, Temperance Unions and the Baptist Union. The Tasmanian Archives also holds records of advocacy bodies such as the Tenants Union of Tasmania[28] and the Tasmanian Council of Social Services (TASCOSS).[29] Whilst not often containing case files, the records of these bodies document changes in social policy and the push for more government involvement with addressing housing concerns.

As far as the lived experience of individuals, the Tasmanian Archives' Community Archives include day books and administration records from both the Hobart Women's Shelter[30] and Caroline House.[31] Caroline House provided supported accommodation from the 1970s to 2021, for women experiencing a range of challenges.

The Tasmanian Archives also has a small number of records from the real estate industry. Whilst not holding any records from the Real Estate Institute of Tasmania, the Archives does include the records of a small number of real estate firms, such as Rupert Johnston Pty Ltd,[32] which operated until 1972, and 'Roberts and Co',[33] which operated in Tasmania from 1865.

Using the Tasmanian Archives

One researcher intimately familiar with Tasmanian Archives' holdings of housing records is the University of Tasmania researcher and lecturer Dr Kathleen Flanagan. Dr Flanagan made extensive use of the post-World War II public housing-related records in the development of her PhD thesis and subsequent 2020 publication *Housing, neo-liberalism and the archive*.[34] Dr Flanagan gives a wonderfully illustrative description of some of the administrative records that have been retained by the Tasmanian Archives:

> … In the Tasmanian 'archive' I found files replete with a …. diverse assortment of documents, most of them with dates and names and positions attached: correspondence received and copies of correspondence sent; internal and external memoranda; the official minutes of meetings, as well as sometimes, the notes of individuals participants; the draft and final versions of Cabinet submissions, sometimes filed along with memos, notes and 'working' documents, all of which can shed light on their development, reception and outcome; file notes ranging from typed formal records of key conversations and processes through to handwritten jottings on scrap paper identified only by an illegible set of initials and a date; photocopies of pages from books or extracts from other files; copies of submissions and statements of policy from non-government agencies or individuals; press releases; internal reports; discussion drafts; briefing notes prepared by more junior staff for their superiors or for the Minister; brochures and information sheets; plans of houses or the layout of the subdivisions; invoices; purchase orders, receipts and other material pertaining to accounts payable and receivable; forms blank and completed; and marginalia of all kinds ….[35]

During a recent discussion,[36] Dr Flanagan stated that she found value in the sets of culled or 'sampled' case files that the Tasmanian Archives has retained. However, she noted having difficulty in using these files to tell the broader story of the operation of the Housing

Department(s) or the Department's impact on their clients. Dr Flanagan described her experience of finding broader administrative and higher-level planning records to be useful. For example, she found that subdivision files with debates over policy development sometimes also included glimpses of individual cases. These files are often quite thick, with much of the paperwork not being relevant. Dr Flanagan noted that the time-consuming process of going through these more dry, administrative records may put off general researchers. For these researchers, case files, such as welfare files, may be a more attractive source of personal stories.

To discover the lived experience of tenants, Dr Flanagan also made use of files, which include records of property maintenance[37] and records of a committee specifically looking at 'eviction and problem cases'.[38] Dr Flanagan stated that the records of this committee were particularly useful in giving her an insight into how government departments categorise and understand people regarded as problematic. Although they include names and addresses of people, the papers of this committee are open for public access. Dr Flanagan expressed concern around this and emphasised that the confidentiality of those included should be maintained by researchers.

Whilst commenting that the voices of tenants were not often found within the available records, Dr Flanagan noted the informative nature of comments included by staff within files. These comments could be seen as demonstrating how the bureaucracy conceptualised and categorised tenants. It is interesting to note feedback that Dr Flanagan received after giving a presentation on her research. Public servants in the audience stated that they could not believe that people in the past had 'written that stuff down'. Perhaps this demonstrates a changing culture where today's government officers are more cautious regarding the opinions and subjective comments they add to official records?

Looking forward – adding to the Archives

When looking for records of 'housing', it can seem obvious that useful information will be found in the records of the housing department(s). However, these departments often have a focus on public housing and retaining the records of this function. Looking more broadly, other agencies and departments of the Government can be found to also play a role in the rental and social housing sectors. Most often, this is in establishing and enforcing regulations or in providing project funding. For example, Tasmanian legislation has been in place since the 1950s to regulate the Real Estate industry.[39] The Auctioneers and Real Estate Agents Council[40] operated under this legislation and heard complaints on professional and ethical conduct. Records of this Council could show another aspect of how housing has been provided to Tasmanians. Retaining at least a selection of their records would achieve the Tasmanian Archives' stated aim to retain records of government accountability and evidence of the affording of rights and entitlements. Unfortunately, these records are not held by the Tasmanian Archives. Despite active correspondence with this Council[41] (which, in 2006, was replaced by the 'Property Agents Board'), the Archives has received none of the Council's records. The only way to review the activities of these bodies is to access the annual reports and newsletters that have been lodged with the State Library. Another set of records that the Tasmanian Archives should receive in the future to shine a light for researchers on the experiences of renters in Tasmania are those of the Residential Tenancy Commissioner. The Commissioner oversees Rental Services,[42] which investigates disputes amongst tenants, property owners and real estate agents, and ensures compliance with statutory obligations.

Disposal Authorisation No. 2501 (DA2501) for the functional records of Housing Tasmania was released by the Tasmanian Archives in 2018.[43] This schedule encompasses Government 'housing'-related records that are currently being created, as well as those post 1960 records ready for archiving or destruction. This schedule covers the functions of Housing Programs, the Housing Portfolio and Supply, Tenancy Services and Emergency response and recovery. The term 'significant' is used in this schedule to guide records managers to those records that should be classified as permanent and sent to Archives. Although the use of the term 'significant' is quite common in disposal schedules, it can be a difficult thing to define and use when sentencing records. DA2501 includes 'plans, summaries of consultation, public submissions which alter a program, final reports and committee records' in the category of significant records of the function of 'Housing Programs'. For the function 'Tenancy Programs', significant records are defined as those that 'document tenancy services matters that set a precedent, lead to a change in policy and/or program design and criteria'. In contrast, records of the people living in the housing including 'detailed records of tenants that required intensive management' are temporary – to be destroyed 100 years after the birth date of the tenant. Other general tenancy management or transactional records are scheduled for destruction seven years after the last tenancy. Currently, in Tasmania, applications for social housing are maintained in a 'Tasmanian Housing Register'. As of December 2020, there were 3813 applications on this register.[44] If this register is interpreted as 'applications for public housing services, determination of eligibility/priority, and correspondence with applicants', then under the current disposal schedule, this register could be a temporary record.

Conclusion

Records in the Tasmanian Archives do not tell the full story of Tasmanians experiencing housing stress and disadvantage. Whilst attempts have been made to be objective and systematic in retaining records related to housing, there are obvious gaps and silences. Broad social norms, personal bias and practical concerns have all influenced decisions around the disposal and retention of some of the key sources of personal housing stories and information such as case files. The Tasmanian Archives has also been shaped by ideas held by archivists and record officers regarding what future researchers may want to access, or on what is considered 'serious' or 'legitimate' research. The Tasmanian Archives' collections have, in addition, been shaped by the structure of the formal government organisation that manages the collection. For example, the amount of resourcing that is given to collection development and proactive collecting directly affects the shape and growth of the collection.

Destroying case files may be justified through both resource management and privacy concerns. They are notoriously voluminous, often repetitive and most contain unremarkable administrative activities. However, what context, content and depth is lost through retaining only final reports, annual reports and summaries of actions taken? What about the stories behind the statistics? How do we access the voices of those affected by policy? How do we show government policy and processes in action? How do we show the reasons for and effects of grass roots community service delivery to address housing scarcity?

Moving forward, Archives Agencies, including the Tasmanian Archives, need to develop disposal schedules and collecting practices that balance practical considerations with the need to have collections which do their best to reflect the Australian community. Included in this is the need to find a way to include individual – messy, repetitive, private and subjective – accounts of lived experience. As quoted at the start of this paper 'Without the patterns and themes uncovered by research in [case files] ... the history of institutions could be told, but not that of people'.[45]

26

Notes on contributor

Jennifer Jerome began her archival journey working with the records and library collection of Adelaide Central Mission (now Uniting Communities). After completing a Master of Information Studies, Jennifer joined the National Archives of Australia, working in both Canberra and Hobart. Since 2007, Jennifer has undertaken a wide range of policy and collection management roles with the Tasmanian Archives at Libraries Tasmania. Since 2018, her focus has been on enhancing the diversity and access of Tasmanian Archives' community archives holdings.

Notes

1. Terry Cook, "Many Are Called, but Few are Chosen': Appraisal Guidelines for Sampling and selecting Case Files', Archivaria, vol. 32, Summer 1991, pp. 25–50.
2. See the International Covenant on Economic, Social and Cultural Rights (ICESCR) article 11 – 'Every person has the right to an adequate standard of living, which includes the right to adequate housing', available at https://www.ohchr.org/en/instruments-mechanisms/instruments/international-covenant-economic-social-and-cultural-rights, accessed 20 September 2023.
3. The Archives Act 1983 (Tasmania) gives the State Archivist the responsibility to retain records that have been designated within Tasmanian legislation as requiring permanent retention. The Act also allows the State Archivist to issue guidelines that assist authorities in determining which of their records are permanent.
4. Tasmanian Government, 'Archives Act 1983', available at https://www.legislation.tas.gov.au/view/html/inforce/current/act-1983-076, accessed 1 September 2022.
5. Tasmanian Government, 'Libraries Act 1984', available at https://www.legislation.tas.gov.au/view/html/inforce/current/act-1984-109, accessed 1 September 2022.
6. Tasmanian Parliament, 'Tasmanian Parliamentary Papers 1856–1901', available at https://www.parliament.tas.gov.au/tpl/PPWeb/, accessed 20 September 2023.
7. Peter R. Eldershaw, Guide to the Public Records of Tasmania: Section 1. Colonial Secretary's Office, Hobart, Archives Office of Tasmania, 1957 (Revised 1988).
8. Tasmanian Archives, 'Charitable Grants Department (TA21), Listing Available at Libraries Tasmania', https://stors.tas.gov.au/AI/TA21, accessed 20 September 2023.
9. Hobart City Council, Houses for the Poor Committee, Minutes of Various Special Committees of the Council, 1904, (Tasmanian Archives: MCC16/70/1/11), available at: https://stors.tas.gov.au/AI/MCC16-70-1-11, accessed 20 September 2023.
10. Ellen Scheinburg, 'Case file theory: Does it work in practice?, Archivaria, vol. 38, Fall 1994, pp. 45–60.
11. Sheila Powell, 'Archival Reappraisal: The Immigration Case Files', Archivaria, vol. 33, Winter 1991, pp. 104–116.
12. National Archives of Australia, 'Disposal Freezes and Retention Notices', available at https://www.naa.gov.au/information-management/disposing-information/disposal-freezes-and-retention-notices, accessed 1 September 2022.
13. Archives Office of Tasmania, Disposal Schedule DS22, Tasmanian Government, Hobart, 1995.
14. Tasmanian Archives, 'Agricultural Bank of Tasmania, Applications for Assistance and Associated Correspondence Under the Housing Department Act 1938 and 1946 (Srd) (AB106), Listing Available at Libraries Tasmania, available at https://stors.tas.gov.au/AI/AB106, accessed 20 September 2023.
15. David Bloomfield, 'Fair Rents Boards – A Necessary Instrument of Social Justice', Tasmanian Historical Research Association Papers and Proceedings, vol.67, no.1, April 2020, pp. 40–55.
16. Tasmanian Archives, 'Fair Rent Boards, Applications Nos. 301–400 for Rent Determinations and Reductions, with Inspection Reports and Associated Papers (AGD41), 1943–1944', Listing Available at Libraries Tasmania, available at https://stors.tas.gov.au/AI/ADG41, accessed 20 September 2023.
17. Tasmanian Archives, 'Agricultural Bank or the Tasmanian Development Authority, Client Files, (AC699), 1946–1998, listing available at Libraries Tasmania', available at https://stors.tas.gov.au/AI/AC699, accessed 20 September 2023.
18. Tasmanian Archives, 'Housing Department, Yellow Back Files for Premises Purchased or Vacated (HD9), 1947–1977, Listing Available at Libraries Tasmania, available at https://stors.tas.gov.au/AI/HD9, accessed 20 September 2023.

19. Tasmanian Archives, 'Hobart Benevolent Society (NG1637), Listing Available at Libraries Tasmania, available at https://stors.tas.gov.au/AI/NG1637, accessed 20 September 2023.

20. Tasmanian Archives, 'Launceston Benevolent Society (NG185), Listing Available at Libraries Tasmania , available at https://stors.tas.gov.au/AI/NG185, accessed 20 September 2023.

21. Tasmanian Archives, 'Burnie Benevolent Society (NG1851). Listing Available at Libraries Tasmania, available at https://stors.tas.gov.au/AI/NG1851, accessed 20 September 2023.

22. Tasmanian Archives, 'Hobart Benevolent Society, Records of the Hobart Benevolent Society (NS1637), 1859–1992, Listing Available at Libraries Tasmania, available at https://stors.tas.gov.au/AI/NS1637, accessed 20 September 2023.

23. Ibid., NS1637/1/6, p. 338

24. Tasmanian Archives, 'Launceston Benevolent Society, Report Book of Inspector (NS185), 1869–1878, Listing Available at Libraries Tasmania, available at https://stors.tas.gov.au/AI/NS185, accessed 20 September 2023.

25. Tasmanian Archives, 'Hobart City Mission, Minutes of Meetings of the Mission 1928–1934 (NS6863/1/7), Listing Available at Libraries Tasmania, available at https://stors.tas.gov.au/AI/NS6863, accessed 20 September 2023.

26. Tasmanian Archives, 'Slum Abolition League, 1940–1945 (NG1303), Listing Available at Libraries Tasmania, available at https://stors.tas.gov.au/AI/NG13103, accessed 20 September 2023.

27. The records of religious organisations held by the Tasmanian Archives can be located by searching for the function of 'Religion', available at https://stors.tas.gov.au/AI/39 , accessed 20 September 2023.

28. Tasmanian Archives, 'Tenants Union of Tasmania (NG2003), Listing Available at Libraries Tasmania, available at https://stors.tas.gov.au/AI/NG2003, accessed 20 September 2023.

29. Tasmanian Archives, 'Tasmanian Council of Social Services (TASCOSS) (NG2278), Listing Available at Libraries Tasmania, available at https://stors.tas.gov.au/AI/NG2278, accessed 20 September 2023.

30. Tasmanian Archives, 'Hobart Women's Shelter (NG721), Listing Available at Libraries Tasmania, available at https://stors.tas.gov.au/AI/NG721, accessed 20 September 2023.

31. Tasmanian Archives, 'Caroline House (NG3564), Listing Available at Libraries Tasmania, available at https://stors.tas.gov.au/AI/NG3564, accessed 20 September 2023.

32. Tasmanian Archives, 'Rupert Johnston Pty Ltd (NG3511), Listing Available at Libraries Tasmania, available at https://stors.tas.gov.au/AI/NG3511, accessed 20 September 2023.

33. Tasmanian Archives, '"Roberts and Co" (NG3312), Listing Available at Libraries Tasmania avaialble at https://stors.tas.gov.au/AI/NG3312, accessed 20 September 2023.

34. Kathleen Flanagan, Housing, Neoliberalism and the Archive: Reinterpreting the Rise and Fall of Public Housing, Routledge, London, 2020.

35. Ibid., p. 10

36. Jennifer Jerome in conversation with Dr Kathleen Flanagan regarding Dr Flanagan's experience of using the Tasmanian Archives to find evidence of the lived experience of Tasmanians, 5 October 2022.

37. For example, Tasmanian Archives, Housing Department, Tenancy and Allotment of Home Files (SRD), 1973 to 1984), (AB371/1/1).

38. Tasmanian Archives, Housing Department, FA4041-SOC/01 - Social Environment Committee-Housing of Eviction and Problem cases, General Correspondence Files – "Fa Files,"(AD668/1/43).

39. Estate Agents Act 1936 (TAS) and Auctioneers and Estate Agents Act 1959 (TAS)

40. Tasmanian Archives, 'The Auctioneers and Real Estate Agents Council (TA1576), Listing Available at Libraries Tasmania, available at https://stors.tas.gov.au/AI/TA1576, accessed 20 September 2023.

41. Archives Office of Tasmania, Correspondence Files Regarding Agencies' Records Disposal and Recordkeeping [Std Files], STD166/1 Auctioneers & Real Estate Agents Council, 1998–2000.

42. Tasmanian Archives, 'Rental Services (TA2142), Listing Available at Libraries Tasmania, available at https://stors.tas.gov.au/AI/TA2142, accessed 20 September 2023.

43. Tasmanian Government, 'Office of the State Archivist, Disposal Authorisation No.2501: Disposal Schedule for Functional Records of Housing Tasmania, 19 June 2018', available at https://www.informationstrategy.tas.gov.au/Publications/Document%20Library%20%20RDS/Housing%20Tasmania%20Records.PDF, accessed 1 September 2022.

44. Jacqueline De Vries, etal., 'The Tasmanian housing market: update 2020–21', Housing and Community Research Unit, University Of Tasmania, June 2021, available at https://www.utas.edu.au/__data/assets/pdf_file/0005/1475465/UOTBR210619-Tasmanian-Housing-Update_vFinal.pdf , accessed 1 September 2022.

45. Terry Cook, op. cit., p. 25.

REFLECTION ARTICLE

Documenting Australian Society – Performing Arts Community of Practice

Jenny Fewster*

Australian Research Data Commons

Abstract

While the performing arts are a vitally important dimension of the cultural life of Australia, the performances themselves are often ephemeral and difficult to document in an enduring form. This article describes a successful, collaborative, community of practice-based model for ensuring the creation and curation of performing arts documentation in Australia. The collaboration involves key national professional and industry organisations and peak bodies, working together to ensure that important documentation is identified, preserved, and made available via the AusStage research and discovery platform.

Keywords: Communities of practice; Performing arts; AusStage; Documentation strategy.

The community responsible for producing, collecting, preserving and researching the performing arts in Australia has become a model for best practice, both in Australia and internationally. The performing arts is a highly ephemeral artform, sometimes with no material trace of its happening after the event. This creates challenges for the accurate recording of the artform for posterity, challenges which have been largely overcome by a strong community working together for the greater good. Performing arts practice is a highly collaborative endeavour, and this is reflected in the community of practice dedicated to documenting it for future generations.

There are three pivotal stakeholders in the performing arts community of practice in Australia. Two professional bodies, the Australasian Association for Theatre, Drama and Performance Studies (ADSA) and the Performing Arts Heritage Network (PAHN) of the Australian Museums and Galleries Association (AMaGA), represent the theatre, drama and performance studies scholars and the performing arts collections custodians, respectively. AusStage, the research and resource discovery platform for Australian live performance, represents the interests of both of these bodies, as well as industry and government, providing a useful focal point for the community.

*Correspondence: Jenny Fewster, Email: jenny.fewster@ardc.edu.au

Australasian Association for Theatre, Drama and Performance Studies, the peak academic association promoting the study of drama in any performing medium throughout Australasia, represents staff and postgraduate students of Australasian institutions of tertiary education who are engaged in teaching, research and practice in theatre, drama and performance studies. Directors of associated theatres and members of the theatrical profession are also active members. ADSA's annual conference is held once a year and attracts delegates from universities, industry, government, and collections.

Performing Arts Heritage Network is a small yet vibrant national network whose members come together in the interests of collecting, preserving, and making accessible Australia's performing arts heritage. Records documenting this rich heritage are found throughout dispersed collections residing in museums, galleries, and libraries both urban and rural. PAHN holds annual conferences that have sought to highlight these dispersed collections and, by emphasising regional and place specific performing arts heritage, to make connections between collections, research, industry, and practitioners.

AusStage is the discipline's research and discovery platform, a sophisticated research tool which documents performing arts productions with integrated associations to data about physical resources. AusStage performs a curatorial function, accumulating a virtual collection of items that are otherwise dispersed in actual collections nationally and internationally. By streamlining discovery in this way, AusStage enables researchers to more easily engage with the rich history and heritage of Australian performing arts and artists, at home and abroad. As a result, AusStage provides improved opportunities for research and education, and increased visibility for libraries, museums, archives, and documentation centres of the performing arts.

AusStage's methodological innovations and data standards were acknowledged in a recent review of digital resources in *Theatre Journal*, the discipline's leading periodical. In it, AusStage is described as one of 'the most sophisticated and promising efforts to develop a digital database for theatre and performance research' with 'broad application' for 'reshaping the way we think about preserving, examining, and cataloging performance ephemera'.[1]

The symbiotic intersection between ADSA, PAHN and AusStage has facilitated relationship-building among the community. Members of PAHN provide AusStage with the source material to create 'thin' data records detailing event information, such as place and time, cast, and creatives. In turn, AusStage provides PAHN members with increased public exposure by recording information about holdings in their collections. Members of ADSA use AusStage to give scholarly interpretation to the data and PAHN holdings in research papers, journal articles, books, and other research outputs.

The organisations also have formalised relationships. The Chair of PAHN has been a partner on every AusStage funding application and holds a position on the Advisory Council. Likewise, ADSA has been represented on each AusStage funding application with the Chair of the Executive holding a position on the Advisory Council. Reciprocally, the Project Manager of AusStage has been a member of PAHN since 2002 and has held a position on the Committee since 2008. The AusStage Manager also holds a position on the ADSA Executive Committee.

Australasian Association for Theatre, Drama and Performance Studies, PAHN and AusStage facilitate, promote, and nurture relationships between stakeholders, forming a coherent, cooperative and collaborative community. The focus on Australian performance histories provides a common passion for professionals from research, collections and industry to explore synergies and opportunities for future collaboration. Many of the members of the community have a background in performance practice, so collaborative practice and working towards collective learning are traits that are well engrained and heartily embraced. There is a tacit understanding that by working together there will be outcomes for the common good in the documentation of performing arts in Australia.

Furthermore, the organisations themselves are driven by the needs of their users. Their governance is derived from their membership base, providing a ground-up approach to leadership. This model of self-governance gives a sense of ownership which creates identity, trust, value, and connection. Practitioners in the community view each other as peers and place value on their shared identity in relation to the performing arts. This ensures that practitioners perceive a high return on the time they invest in participating in the community.[2]

The community coordinates the annual ADSA and PAHN conferences, and the triennial AusStage symposium which allow the members to meet, share, discuss, collaborate, and evolve; these face-to-face events are enthusiastically attended. Communication in between conferences is less formalised but regular bulletins keep the membership up to date without becoming overwhelming. Informal communication between members is common and is encouraged.

The ephemeral nature of live performance is a contributing factor to the success of the community, not the impediment some might think it to be. Work in performing arts heritage is often about rendering tacit knowledge explicit, making tangible the intangible, and capturing, validating, and documenting that which may otherwise be forgotten. Our community members are storytellers whose stories are about the practice of story-telling. Together AusStage, ADSA and PAHN provide a supportive platform for these stories to be rehearsed, shared, and re-told.

Notes on contributor

Jenny Fewster, is the Humanities Arts and Social Sciences and Indigenous Research Data Commons Director at the Australian Research Data Commons in Adelaide. She began working on performing arts databases in the early 1990s in her role as Research Assistant at the Performing Arts Collection of South Australia. She joined AusStage, the Australian national online resource for live performance research, when the project began in 2000 and was appointed Project Manager in 2003. During her time with AusStage the project was successful in gaining over $4 million (AUD) in funding from the Australian Research Council, Australian National Data Service, National eResearch Architecture Taskforce, eResearch South Australia and the Australian Access Federation.

Notes

1. D Caplan, 'Notes from the Frontier: Digital Scholarship and the Future of Theatre Studies', *Theatre Journal*, vol. 67, no.2, 2015, pp. 357–358.
2. Etienne and Beverley Wenger-Trayner, *Introduction to Communities of Practice: A Brief Overview of the Concept and Its Uses*, 2015, available at: https://www.wenger-trayner.com/wp-content/uploads/2022/06/15-06-Brief-introduction-to-communities-of-practice.pdf accessed 31 July 2023.

REFLECTION ARTICLE

Honouring Stories of Struggle: Reassessing Australia's Records of Disadvantage – Hearing the Voices of Those Who Struggle

Robyn Sutherland*

Uniting Communities, Adelaide, Australia

Abstract

When deciding what and how documentation should be made and kept about the experiences of welfare recipients, it is vital to ensure that recordkeeping strategies meet the needs, preferences and expectations of the recipients of those services. This article presents a transcription of a video created by a non-government community welfare organisation in South Australia that features interviews with a range of that organisation's clients. Interviewees express concern about the partial and overly negative view of their life experiences captured in the documentation of welfare provision. They suggest that a more holistic approach to documenting their lives would preserve a more accurate and humanistic record of their stories of struggle.

Keywords: *Community welfare*; *Recordkeeping*; *Non-government organisation*

Note: This is a transcription of a video presented at the UNESCO Australian Memory of the World Documenting Australian Society symposium, 'Honouring the Stories of Struggle' hosted by the National Archives of Australia in Canberra on 21 October 2022. Transcription prepared by Rachel Watson.

My name is Robyn Sutherland and I am the Executive Manager of Community Services at Uniting Communities. Uniting Communities is a large, not-for-profit non-government community welfare organisation that provides services to many thousands of people across South Australia.

When I was first asked to present at this seminar, it took me a while to get my head around how I would have anything useful to say. I thought about archiving in a very generalist sense. As I thought about it, I realised that our organisation has been around for nearly 115 years and, in fact, for 115 years what we have been doing is collecting people's stories and archiving their information. I then had to ask myself, were we actually honouring the stories of people and the information that they give to us?

*Correspondence: Robyn Sutherland Email: robyn.sutherland@unitingcommunities.org

Archives & Manuscripts 2023, 51(1): 10961 - http://dx.doi.org/10.37683/asa.v51.10961

Like most organisations, we collect a lot of information. It needs to meet the criteria of the Privacy Act, it has to meet legislation and it needs to meet the requirements of the government bodies that fund us. It has to meet the requirements for how we want to use information in the organisation. And as I thought about that, I realised that, for most people that come to our organisation, they are usually very marginalised. Sometimes for those people, it might be a one-off interaction and we never see them again. But predominantly for most people, organisations such as ours or government agencies we have been collecting their information and archiving it, all their lives. Sometimes for the lives of their family members and their parents.

The information that we gather is problem saturated and only shows the stories of those people while they're interacting with us. It doesn't honour who they are the other 90% of the time that they're not interacting with us. I then thought that it was important that I went out and started talking to people and asking them what they understood about the information that was being collected about them, what that said about them and whether they would have an interest in telling their full story about who they are.

I then started looking at our data; how many requests do we receive from people wanting to access their files? I looked at a period of time of 12 months; it was through COVID so it probably was a lot less, but we had 200 requests for files to be accessed. Eighty-five percent of those requests were coming from government; from child protection, and it was very much looking for information probably to have children removed – whether it was right or wrong, it was that snippet. Only 13 people asked to access their file just out of interest to find out what was being collected about them. I was quite shocked – and then the more that I asked people did they understand what was being collected about them, many people didn't. What they said is because we were explaining how we collect and use information at the beginning of their journey with us they were at the heart of crisis and not always hearing.

I then talked to staff to find out from them, do we collect the whole story? In fact, most of the information that we collect is about trauma, sadness, crisis and hurt. Very little is collected about people when things are going well, because when things are going well, people leave us and we stop collecting it.

I thought what would be most useful in my presentation for this seminar is for you to hear from the voices of people who are marginalised. I went to two different groups and in those two groups are people who interact with the Child Protection System and those who come through our Drug and Alcohol Services. What I know about them is that they've probably had people collecting information about them all of their lives, and I thought what would be more useful is hearing from them, hearing their stories. And as I spoke to people and as you hear these stories, people wanted to talk about the moment, what was going on for them now, what had gone on for them while they were interacting with services like ours. I wanted to try and steer people away from that and talk about whether they want to share their whole story, but I think the thing that we do have to think about is for these people, collecting their stories has had a negative connotation, they kept talking about 'it's the negativeness, it's not who I am'. It is so important for people to talk about what that meant for them, and then once they talked about that process there was this real passion for wanting people to know the full story. But we never ask people what information they want us to collect about them. When they leave our services, we don't ask them 'what else do you want to tell us about yourself' and that's a really interesting question. We need to be thinking about that in the process of how we collect information. Here are a few snippets of the interviews that we've conducted. I wonder what questions it will have you asking yourself about how do we collect information. How do we collect stories, and what do we want to do with them?

'No mandala could tell my story'.

'What you'd have on the paper wouldn't reflect anything of what I've done in my life'.

'The collection of information, I don't feel tells the whole story of who I am'.

'Sometimes you'll mention something and it gets focussed on in the wrong way, like maybe it looks more important on paper than it actually is in my life'.

'I guess unfortunately the majority of the data that has been collecting in regards to myself, it's negative'.

'I really do think it's important for me to share my whole story'.

'My story is about overcoming adversity'.

'I'd like to think there was some nice things said about me. Unless it's just from the initial interview – and if it's just from the initial interview I don't even remember doing it because I was in active addiction at that point in time and I was probably drunk. So it just depends on when and where they were taking that information and whether they keep taking notes as you improve during the program or how it works, I'm not 100% sure'.

'I don't know where my data is I don't even know completely what is collected. I don't know who wants to use it, I don't know who can use my data'.

'I actually have folders full of education results and accomplishments and achievements in my life that nobody would look at'.

'People have been collecting information for probably the last 10 years'.

'So over the past year there's been a lot of information collected about me and my family there's been Mental Health services drug and alcohol rehabilitation services, Department of Child Protection, several Uniting Communities programs, Metropolitan Youth Health, Legal Commissions. I have no idea about the data that's collected on me or who it has been shared with or where it goes – I just know I've been asked a lot of questions in the past year'.

'I think people have been collecting data and information about me since the day I was born. I guess the minute I came out of the womb or maybe when I was still in the womb actually. So, all of that is still on record'.

'When I've gone to get help… that's the records that everybody's got. They come out and were used against me in a bad way, a really bad way, and used against my children. My children were split up in different houses all over the place'.

'Well, the current information they have on me makes me look like it's just about drugs and alcohol and problems with substance and this and that. But I've achieved a lot more than that in my life and you know, obviously that's not recorded'.

'Moving on I'm a completely different person to what I was two years ago, you know, I'm just not that person anymore. And it is hard because all that information that's going to be held on me is all based on the negatives and of extreme parts of my life from when I was in a terrible place, you know. So, they're always going to be over my head, and yeah, it's hard.

I'd really like a nice clean slate now, you know in some aspects of things but I'd also like to... well my stories can be useful as well, you know, but not necessarily as defining who I am now, because I'm not that person anymore'.

'Going over all the information that has been collected about me, some of the times that it's affected me negatively getting a job, it didn't really represent me and who I am properly. The data that was collected, it showed a bad light on me without looking at me as a person and who I am, it was just looking at one event one time where I might have made a mistake. And that stopped me, or could have stopped me, from getting employment'.

'My understanding of the information that's been collected about me now is different to what it was when it was collected. I didn't understand it until it was used against me in court and the youth courts. Then when they collected all the information from all the services that I'd used over the years and presented to me and presented to the courts I couldn't believe that that was the picture that was kind of collated of me, and that was how I was perceived by the courts. I had lots of files at home and references from employers and really good stuff but none of that was looked at. The stuff that was looked at was stuff from different services that I'd gone into when I was in a real hard way, a bad way, and needed food for my family or needed housing or things were going bad and I'd gone into these different services looking for help and I had to present myself as in a bad way. So, when I went to the youth courts there was all this paperwork saying that I was constantly in a bad way and it wasn't accurate. It wasn't an accurate portrayal of my life'.

'Nobody's asked me about the things that I've wanted to say, they've all demanded that I answered the questions that they wanted to hear'.

'I think stories about people like myself would be very important to collect and the whole picture, you know, not just those negative events, the whole entire thing'.

'I think there'd be great value in hearing my story and what I've been through'.

'I think there's a point in recording my story'.

'If somebody was to ask me about my story they should literally just ask me, 'well, how do you see yourself?''

'Who I am now, I'm a mum, a stay-at-home mum who also works as a disability support worker or in the aged care sector. I am a good person, I try to be a good person, very much so. I've learnt from my mistakes, I want my children to see me being a good person. I want hopefully for them to learn from my mistakes'. 'If I was asked to share my story I would probably be interested in that. I suppose for me the comebacks are always bigger than the setbacks. Every time I've fallen I've gotten up and achieved a lot more than I had, and especially this time around in my recovery journey, my comeback has been full of positives that would be wonderful to share and could help a lot of other struggling addicts out there'.

'Who would benefit from hearing my story? I just believe that whoever's in charge of the youth courts could really use some help, like in structuring their system a bit better, they really need to listen to people that are in the system, but they know and then not think that because they've got University educations that they're somehow high and mighty and superior and brush off people that maybe are criticising their actions. Well maybe not criticising their actions, we want to be heard and we want them to take note of what we're saying and to just give options, to make better options'.

'If someone was to record my entire life story to get the real picture of who I am today, I would want to share all the bits, good, bad everything because all of that is who I am, that defines me, the good and the bad, the whole picture. If I leave bits out it's not going to make a lot of sense is it?'

'As far as sharing my story and adding that to the archives, I'd be absolutely…that would be brilliant to do. I mean, as far as my journey going forward from this program, the jobs that I'm going to be looking at doing is going to be a lot based on my life experience so I'm going to archive that regardless of whether someone wants me to do it for the archives because I'm going to have that in my resume. My life story's going to be part of my resume and all the stuff that I've done and working with Indigenous people and working in drug and alcohol and, you know, being a chef and having apprentices and running large teams of people as a manager, all that stuff's going to go into my story and I'm going to write it, whether someone asks me to do it or not. So that's going to be part of me creating my resume to move forward into what I want to do'.

'Who am I all alright; who I am is I'm a nice, caring, good person who just wants to be involved in society and has missed a lot through his life and has made many, many, many mistakes but knows he's made these mistakes and I know that I can be a massive contribution to something. I don't know what, you know, I can be very helpful, whether it's in this organisation or the art world or I just don't know. But I think I've got heaps of potential that was definitely muffled by my choices of drugs etc and in life. That's who I am and that's what I wish people knew about me is where I'm sort of headed and who I am now, and not of those terrible times they were in my life where I mean, geez, I was sometimes suicidal in my life or I had to come to a breaking point before I got to becoming wanting to become good. But I've never felt so good about myself in my life and never been as happy as I am now and just to my thirst for knowledge and my brain's all opening up and everything and, you know, I was just dumbed down, you know, for a long time, you know. I didn't have any confidence, the loss of self-esteem as well, you know, Now I'm just ready, I'm really, really happy, you know, just ready to take on everything. But, yeah, I definitely think that my information like when I went to court the other day, I was saying, I had all these letters of, carried references in that from Uniting Communities drug and alcohol rehabilitation and prevention service and everything else and the judge actually stopped and commended me on it, you know. Which was good but whereas if I hadn't had all those letters and that, my history would have looked terrible, you know. But yeah, then he was obviously glad that I gave him that information so then it was good, yeah'.

Going through this whole process for me really has me questioning the way we collect information. I know that we do it in the way that meets privacy and meets all the legislative requirements, but I feel that we're actually missing the most important thing about people, which is about their resilience and their whole story. That we're only getting one bit and so certainly what I'm taking away from this is that I think we're going to start to look at the way we collect information. At the heart of it, or at least when people are leaving our services, ask them 'what else do you want to tell us about yourself?'

REFLECTION ARTICLE

Building a Participatory Archive With an Australian Suburb: Case Study of Canberra's Biggest Bogan Suburb, Kambah

Louise Curham*

Libraries, Archives, Records & Information Science, iSchool@School of Media, Creative Arts & Social Inquiry, Curtin University, Perth, Australia

Abstract

Participatory appraisal and building archives with communities have been discussed amongst archivists across the world for decades. There is reportage on building community resources for and by Aboriginal and Torres Strait Islander communities, but there is less reportage on these endeavours with other communities. This reflection reports on building an archive with the community of Kambah, a suburb with a mixed reputation in the Canberra community.

A challenge for participatory archives identified through this project was scale – if successful, the volume of content quickly becomes overwhelming. Another challenge is the responsibility that goes with accepting content from contributors. Expectations are set up that the content will be used or shared. And crucially, participation means everyone. Strategies are needed to connect with contributors that go beyond relationships in easy reach for the archivist based on existing connections.

A final lesson comes from socially engaged art, a practice that focuses on community participation. This calls on the archivist to recognise their standpoint, the worldview they bring. Our sector has recognised that collections and building them is not neutral. For archivists, there remains much to do to work out how to meaningfully share that power and authority as collections are built.

Keywords: *Community archives*; *Participatory appraisal*; *Participatory archives.*

This article is a reflection about a project in the suburbs of Canberra that innovates in terms of its method for building a community archive by drawing on practices from socially engaged art. Its findings are provisional as the project is ongoing.

In January 2023, a project to build a digital community resource to depict life in Kambah was shared with the Canberra public in an exhibition called 'Kambah' at the Tuggeranong Arts Centre, an Australian Capital Territory (ACT) Government gallery in south Canberra.[1] This exhibition investigated the experience of living in Kambah, reported as a suburb with low social capital and known on the internet as one of Australia's biggest bogan suburbs.[2] I have been living in Kambah for 10 years, involved in the community as a resident in a housing

*Correspondence: Louise Curham Email: louise.curham@curtin.edu.au

development that began as a 1970s co-op and through environment volunteering.[3] Kambah is on the southwest edge of Canberra bordered by one of Australia's most significant rivers, the Murrumbidgee, and Canberra's landmark mountain range, the Brindabellas. Residents consistently report a strong connection with nature.[4]

The suburb Kambah carries the name of the Bennet family station, resumed in 1968 for the new suburb, farmed by Canberra establishment figure Sim Bennet from 1940. Before that, there were a string of owners, documented in work by historian and Kambah resident, Glenn Schwinghamer. This area of the limestone plains is not known as a place where Ngunawal people stayed, but it was a place of passing through and along to other parts of the yam daisy fields and the Murrumbidgee River corridor, part of the Ngunawal estate.[5]

In the late 1960s, much thought went into the planning of Kambah, an example is a 1968 community seminar.[6] Kambah was part of the ACT Government strategy of interspersed public and private housing. When it was established in the 1970s, cheap housing was the norm. The whole of the Tuggeranong Valley, the district Kambah is situated in, became known as 'Nappy Valley', home to many young families.[7] None of these ingredients mark Kambah out as significantly different from other parts of Canberra that were developed in the 1970s and bogan status is fought out on the internet with other suburbs of the same era.[8] Furthermore, being bogan can be both a badge of pride and a pejorative.[9] But the real issue for Kambah is that lack of social capital means our 'glue' is weak enough that we have lost many community assets while other suburbs in Canberra have retained them.[10] In discussion with residents, I learned that many feel they live the 'good life' and feel there is much to value about Kambah.[11] Yet that expression of what they feel is valuable is not made public or shared. This exhibition sought to share a developing collection of residents' experiences. I gathered this reportage in a digital map as images, video, audio recordings and text that taken together are emerging as a community archive. This collection embodies a worldview that collections reflect values and therefore community aspirations.[12]

About the exhibition and Kambah's provenance

The exhibition ran for 2 months in early 2023. It drew on my mixed disciplinary background in archives and media art. Visitors to the gallery engaged with archives through the digital map. My practice using obsolete media to make creative works was shared through a group of my pinhole photographs of Kambah. Digital copies of these are included in map entries.[13] The digital map was displayed on a screen, with a QR code to connect users to it on their mobile phones.

A purpose of the exhibition was to develop entries for the map. The exhibition included a series of public events to tell Kambah residents about the map and seek their contributions: a face-to-face meeting of the Kambah community Facebook group, a walk with a local historian around what remains of Kambah station, a community discussion about government plans to increase housing in Kambah and an inaugural meeting of artists from Kambah and the wider area. Each event was a community gathering in its own right, but there were also opportunities to tell people about the map and seek entries from them.

The digital map began during the COVID-19-induced lockdown that occurred in Canberra in 2020. Funded by a small ACT Arts grant, the digital mapping tool I use was created by two artists, primarily for use with a mobile phone while on the move in the location.[14] It combines video, audio, text and images into entries. It uses a web browser that means no app downloads or log-ins are required. The format options allow a wide range of digital objects to be included, including digital items from public collections like the Canberra District Historical Society and the National Library newspaper collection.

Archives & Manuscripts 2023, 51(1): 10959 - http://dx.doi.org/10.37683/asa.v51.10959

Rules of engagement

I learnt that Kambah has low social capital. This means the relationships and networks amongst residents are not strong. This was reported in research from 2007.[15] I wanted to find out how documenting our experience both in the present and from the past, might help bring us together and build our social capital. I recognised that this experience documentation needed to be gathered. A meaningful way to do this for the community was by locating experiences on a map. I have explained that the digital map involves making entries based on accounts of community members. These are supported by photos of places, events and items such as cookbooks or school memorabilia. I also explained that I have added to this through my consultation with heritage collections that contain material relevant to Kambah. Like notes for file, the accounts from community members are reports of experiences of Kambah. Their authority lies in their link to lived experience and the credentials of the speaker as a resident, alumni or visitor to Kambah. My endeavour was to gather and report what was told to me.

The archivist as broker, the archival conversation

My method to build entries has evolved. To gather entries, initially I made appointments with community leaders such as a member of the region's community council, a politician and a long-term community activist. I also made coffee dates with long-time community members known to me through environment volunteering. My invitation to them was to help me map our experience of Kambah and to share with me what they know about Kambah that others may not. Initially, many people drew a blank in response to my question 'what's important to you about Kambah?'. The question evolved to 'what do you know about Kambah that others may not know that you'd like to share with the community?'. In conversation, I was able to flesh out that I was interested in their attitudes (*I like this but not this*) and their qualitative accounts of experience (*that was scary, that was fun*).

The map as an archives

To get started I made entries based on the work of my historian friend, Glenn Schwinghamer, focused on the pastoral history of the blocks that are now Kambah. I also made entries for some places of particular significance for me such as the cockatoo roosts amongst mature yellow box and red gum lining the old road to the Murrumbidgee river.

There are two features to the map entries. The first is connecting the story to an image. Building an image into the entries allows an interpretation of the social facts recounted in the stories. Some of the images are records, for example brochures of land releases and government promotional material. Others are aesthetic responses and artworks. For example, several of the stories are accompanied by my pinhole photographs. The pinhole process produces an image that is not only faithful to the scene it captures but also upside and back to front; thus it contains both the one-for-one evidence of a physical place but also an interpretation, allowing more than one interpretation.

The second feature of the map entries is that their development requires having conversations. I showed would-be contributors the map and I built on the question 'what do you know that others may not' with the qualifier that their contribution can be tiny or seemingly insignificant. I emphasised that negative stories are also important. Often, the conversations began with the comment, 'I don't think I've got anything worth hearing about'. Ten minutes into the conversation something was uncovered that we both recognised as valuable to others. Some conversations stayed general and no specific event or story emerged, thus no content for the map.

I quickly realised the limitation of my networks and I sought out social workers in the area to explore how I could broaden my conversations. That phase of accompanying the social work team on their public events has not yet taken place. The next phase that has been successful was to use the 8 weeks of the exhibition to have conversations with visitors to the exhibition and public events I described above.

Retelling as a method, standpoint

My role as the broker archivist was to report on what the community shared with me in a way that reflected the responsibility of receiving contributor's stories. Questions I began with included who am I to bring this together? Can I speak on behalf of my community? I used a model of retelling. It is clear that the authorship of the map lies with me; that this is my reportage of the community's experiences. For example, entries built on historian Glenn Schwinghamer's work spell out I am reporting back on what Glenn shared with me. My intention is to pass on the standpoint of contributors, to participate in this exchange as a broker. It is tempting to use the word conduit, but that image of a smooth, frictionless pipe ignores the sticky, personal nature of interpretation. As Jay Phillips writes about Indigenist standpoint theory,[16] drawing on Maggie Walter's 2006 description, this starts with the question 'where does my knowledge come from and what is its purpose and impact'.[17] It starts with taking stock of what has shaped the views and knowledge you have. That place of recognition is the first step in supporting change or development in those knowledge and views.

In making entries, I need to think through the consequences of putting different knowledge in the community side by side. A question I grappled with is how must entries be put together so contributions are visible in an appropriate way? For example, I attempted to have a conversation with community members about Kambah's reputation as bogan. Some residents were totally unaware of this reputation and my perception was they were affronted by it. For others that reputation is fun and playful. For others, it came from a particular time and place. But how to put that into a map entry is a complex problem – for archivists, the question is what are the records that would document 'being bogan'?

What follows are some examples of experiences community members shared with me. They include some context about the story and some reflections from me on how these contributed to it.

Some examples of community experience

25c durries at the Livingstone Street shops
Canberra has a practice of building local shops into the design of suburbs, a practice included in the design of Kambah. These shops have mixed fates over time, some thrive and others fall into disrepair. The Livingstone Street shops recently were turned over to residential development. But in conversation with a former Kambah resident, I asked him what he might know that others might not – he shared that you used to be able to buy single cigarettes at these shops. For me, this was exactly the kind of anecdote I was hoping to draw out. For me, it shines a light on a whole social history of smoking, of a time when a single cigarette was worth buying and selling.

The first computer lab in an ACT government school
A resident shared with me how her husband had introduced computers to one of the Kambah primary schools. Working in the industry, he was able to provide them cheap. The school welcomed that initiative and brought those computers into the classrooms. For me, this shines a light on a different kind of relationship between families and schools that has

operated in the past. It also runs contrary to the perception of our community in Kambah as uncouth and unpolished reflected in that bogan reputation. We had the first computers in our schools.

The drag strip at the tip
Canberra has a system of parks that protect the hills dotted throughout the city, a network known as the Canberra nature parks. Kambah has one of these on its western edge that was home to a tip well into the 1980s. A resident shared with me that the drive towards the tip was a spot he used for some informal rally car driving.

The tip
There were interesting accounts of the tip. It was a foraging site for some; others described accompanying parents who would back up vehicles and offload a huge variety of items including chemicals and paint into the tip pit.

The mid-winter fire-cracker bonfire night
Several people reported on the community bonfire night that took place in mid-winter on a park on one edge of Kambah. It came about as a way for households to incinerate garden waste and other burnables and it doubled as a firecracker night.

Vic and Rick's
I knew our local grocery story by its franchise name, IGA. But I soon realised the community knows it as Vic and Rick's who were the proprietors for decades from the 1980s. Stories included that one of the pair was generous with kids' lollies; the other was tough on kids shopping without parents.

So what are the lessons?
This project connects with our discourse about putting the archivist in service to the community,[18] turning the archivist into a broker between the community and its keeping practices. So, this means inviting the community to recognise the value of their own experience and to think about what might be useful in the future from their stories. My solution to the problem of the neutral archivist is to make my authorship clear and to use a model of re-telling.

Within my question 'is there something about Kambah you know that you would like other people to know', I wanted to extend my community's understanding of what can be archives and how we can build our shared understanding of our place and our community, not just through objects and documents we recognise as heritage, but through individual stories of experience.

So, what did I learn from this that is useful for others seeking to build community archives with communities?

Scale – A backlog quickly built up
I learnt that from a practical standpoint, the number of stories quickly became overwhelming. I built up a backlog of entries that remain several months later. Conversations take time and expectations are established. Initially, I expected success felt like as much engagement as possible with my community, but I realised this generated a problematic backlog. Each engagement involved establishing a relationship, one that was undermined by just gathering stories and adding them to the backlog. In practice, I dealt with the backlog in two ways – I have a 'future contacts' list for those I will follow up and there is a Kambah people's map 'scrapbook', a public-facing blog I use to jot notes relevant to future entries.[19]

Getting past people like me, not just the good times
This project moves incredibly slowly as my understanding of its methods develops. I am seeking to build a resource for and with my community. When participation is invited, an expectation is established in the minds of contributors that their contribution will be honoured and included. My questions include do they want it? What do they want to see in it? I have explained that I take a retelling approach where I report what I hear or learn from my point of view with no attribution to the story contributor. This means my role as a broker is visible and the map is authored by me. In addition to drawing on Indigenist standpoint theory, this takes its lead from socially engaged art, which Frasz and Sidford authoritatively define as creative practice 'that aims to improve conditions in a particular community or in the world' including those of disenfranchised communities. It goes by many names: 'art and social justice, artistic activism, community-based art, cultural organizing, participatory art, relational aesthetics, civic practice, and social practice art'.[20] There has been discussion about the position of artists in these works. Tom Finkelpearl chooses the language 'social co-operation' because these works involve 'a self-identified artist who can claim the title of initiator or orchestrator of the cooperative venture'.[21] As the map grows, it will become clearer if this boundary is more on the side where I lead and the community contributes, in which case more accurate language will be 'participatory'.

Not just the good news
A further challenge is the reportage of good news. A challenge was to get reportage of other kinds of experience. This was limited to a single report of a distressing experience in the 1980s of a male exposing himself to a young horse rider.

Census data show there is a mix in our socio-economics and like much of 1970s Canberra, we have a well-planned mix of public and private housing.[22] Not everyone is enjoying the environment and getting involved in seasonal street parties (although many stories shared with me reflect this). Community leaders working in schools and as social workers alluded to this mixed reality although none of these people belonged to these stories. Illegal activity was another area where some stories were shared, like accounts of the 'munchies' houses a former pizza delivery driver told me about where people would order lots of pizza to round out their marijuana smoking. To find ways to visualise stories like this without necessarily pinpointing them on the map is an interesting challenge.

Future directions
There is much to do to make the entries from the community stories gathered through the exhibition in early 2023. The challenges are working out how to use the media affordances of the map to tell those stories in ways that retell accurately and respectfully. Also crucial is remaining mindful that these stories need to live together in the map with stories of the whole community. There is also more to do to tease out what socially engaged art can offer discussions of community archives.

Acknowledgements
This project was supported by ArtsACT and the Tuggeranong Arts Centre.

Notes on contributor
Louise Curham explores the creative application of old media. Trained in archives, film and time-based art, Louise is a lecturer in the School of Media, Creative Arts and Social Inquiry at Curtin University in Perth, Australia. Her research outputs flow from her work in media art specialising in obsolete technology.

44

Notes

1. 'Kambah', exhibition at Tuggeranong Arts Centre, Jan to Feb 2023, exhibition information, available at https://www.tuggeranongarts.com/events/lousie-curham-kambah/, accessed 1 June 2023.
2. Kambah Peoples Map, 'Top Bogan Suburb?', 2 March 2022, available at https://kambahpeoplesmap.tumblr.com/post/677655112432467968/top-bogan-suburb, accessed 1 June 2023.
3. Urambi Village began as a co-op, with the first houses built in 1976, see 'About Urambi' on the Urambi Village website, available at https://www.urambivillage.com/, accessed 1 June 2022. I have been a con venor of a volunteer group in the ACT Parks and Conservation ParkCare Network, Urambi Hills Group, since 2014, see Urambi Hills Group on Facebook, available at https://www.facebook.com/urambihillsgroup.
4. Kambah Peoples Map, 'Notes from "kitchen table conversation" Kambah 2050, Feb 2023', 1 Mar 2023, available at https://kambahpeoplesmap.tumblr.com/post/710590858879238144/notes-from-kitchen-table-conversation-kambah, accessed 1 June 2023.
5. Ngunawal man Wally Bell has shared publicly about Ngunawal relationships with Kambah in in two public events on Urambi Hills (2015 and 2020), a Kambah park, see, for example, Urambi Hills Facebook events 24 May 2015, 'Aboriginal Heritage Walk', available at https://www.facebook.com/events/1008961625788124, accessed 1 June 2023. I draw my spelling 'Ngunawal' from conversations with Wally Bell.
6. Kambah Peoples Map, 'Tuggeranong Sociological Seminar', 22 Feb 2021, available at https://kambahpeoplesmap.tumblr.com/post/643821817128157184/tuggeranong-sociological-seminar-1969, accessed 1 June 2023.
7. 'Good Times Tuggeranong – More Than Just a Nappy Valley', *The Canberra Times,* 24 November 1988, p. 38, available at http://nla.gov.au/nla.news-article110616171, accessed 1 June 2023.
8. The Riot Act, 'Australia's Top Bogan Suburb – They Name a Few in Canberra!, 4 Aug 2009, available at https://the-riotact.com/australia%E2%80%99s-top-bogan-suburb-they-name-a-few-in-canberra/13177, accessed 1 June 2023.
9. This was reported in discussion with a Kambah resident during the exhibition 'Kambah'.
10. Pierre Bourdieu's definition of social capital applies, 'a durable network ... of mutual acquaintance and recognition ... which provides the backing of ... collectively owned capital', see Pierre Bourdieu, 'The Forms of Capital', in John G. Richardson (ed.), Handbook of Theory and Research for the Sociology of Education, Greenwood Press, NY, 1986, p. 249. The Concerned Residents of West Kambah report, 'Learning from our land – a visionary strategy for West Kambah' includes a definition of social capital, 'increased skills, better networking and improved knowledge of the local community', p. 47. To learn more about assets lost in Kambah see Kambah Peoples Map, 'How did Urambi Primary Turn into Marigal Gardens Instead of a Community Hub?', 11 Feb 2021, available at https://kambahpeoplesmap.tumblr.com/post/642822005235826688/how-did-urambi-primary-turn-into-marigal-gardens, accessed 1 June 2023.
11. Kambah Peoples Map, Notes from 'kitchen table conversation'.
12. An article that eloquently discusses the power of archives as collections is Joan M Schwartz and Terry Cook, 'Archives, Records, and Power: The Making of Modern Memory', Archival Science, vol. 2, no. 1–2, March 2002, pp. 1–19. doi: 10.1007/BF02435628.
13. The exhibition included cyanotypes, a photographic process that dates from 1706, see Christina Anderson, 'Cyanotype: The Blueprint in Contemporary Practice', Routledge, London, New York, 2019, p. 4.
14. Urambi Project, CGEO Maps, available at https://cgeomap.eu/urambi/, CGEO tool created by Fred Adam and Geert Vermeire. See also Mike Duggan and Christina Kiminami, 'Reflecting on Locative Media Art with Fred Adam and Geert Vermeire', Living Maps Network, available at https://www.livingmaps.org/fred-adam-and-geert-vermeire, accessed 1 June 2023.
15. The report, Concerned Residents of West Kambah, 'Learning From Our Land – A Visionary Strategy for West Kambah', 2007 is in the ACT Libraries network and can be available at https://drive.google.com/file/d/1svaDXmpGC_84VRPRrAqdAa71MhYX4GhY/view?usp=sharing, accessed 1 June 2023.
16. Jay Phillips, 'Indigenous Australian studies, Indigenist standpoint pedagogy, and student resistance', in George Noblit (ed), *Oxford Research Encyclopedia of Education*, Oxford University Press, UK, 2019.
17. Maggie Walter, Social Research Methods: An Australian Perspective, Oxford University Press, Melbourne, 2006, p. 11.
18. The scene for this article is set by literature on building archives with communities, notably from Kirsten Thorpe (2017), Lyndon Ormond-Parker and Robyn Sloggett (2012) and Leisa Gibbons (2020). It is also informed by literature on appraisal, processes that result in what gets selected as archives, from Terry Cook (2013), Caswell, Cifor and Ramirez (2016) and Stevens, Flinn and Shepherd (2010).
19. Kambah Peoples Map, blog, available at https://kambahpeoplesmap.tumblr.com/, accessed 1 June 2023.

20. Alexis Frasz and Holly Sidford, 'Mapping the Landscape of Socially Engaged Artistic Practice', in Art Making Change, Helicon Collaborative, 2014, p. 4, available at https://heliconcollab.net/wp-content/uploads/2022/08/FINAL-art-making-change-report_092517.pdf, accessed 1 June 2023.
21. Tom Finkelpearl, What We Made: Conversations on Art and Social Cooperation, Duke University Press, Durham, London, 2013, p. 6.
22. Australian Bureau of Statistics, 'Kambah 2021 Census All Persons, Quick Stats', available at https://www.abs.gov.au/census/find-census-data/quickstats/2021/SAL80082, accessed 1 June 2023.

REFLECTION ARTICLE
COVID-19: What Needs to be Documented? Insights from the Pneumonic Influenza of 1918–1919[1]

Anthea Hyslop*

Abstract

This article compares the influenza pandemic of 1918–1919 and the recent COVID-19 pandemic in their Australian manifestations, with particular reference to their advent and impact, the response of medical science to each, and their management by federal and state authorities. It also comments on the availability of primary sources, both oral and written, for the study of each pandemic ordeal.

Keywords: *Influenza pandemic*; *Documentation strategies*; *Medical science*.

I think I always assumed that the next great pandemic after that of pneumonic influenza would reflect its predecessor in several ways: chiefly in how a society handles the practical problem of very large numbers of people falling sick at once, from a highly infectious and often lethal disease. We would see governments in conference, emergency hospitals established, social activities curbed, local relief measures organised, and of course a vaccine, as soon as one could be devised and deployed. But also, and notwithstanding the emergence some years back of severe acute respiratory syndrome (SARS) and one or two other new diseases, I thought that some sinister variant of the well-known influenza virus was still the likeliest candidate for a pandemic role. And I took it for granted that Australia would not be able to protect itself as it had done in 1918, by strict maritime quarantine measures. That barrier had kept the lethal 'flu' out of the community for almost 3 months, while preparations were made and the virus became somewhat less aggressive. But these days travel by air, so much swifter than by sea, could bring a disease here even before its symptoms had appeared and in any case could hardly be controlled as shipping could. Moreover, our old coastal quarantine stations had long since become museums. As for land quarantine, I don't recall even wondering if our states would close their borders against each other this time around: that kind of thing belonged to another era.

I was near enough right about the practical responses to the community crisis, although the prolonged border closures and the recurrent lockdowns of entire communities, to curb COVID-19, exceeded in severity the movement controls introduced in 1918–1919 against the 'flu'. The initial rejection of face masks for community use surprised me: despite some criticism, they had proved their worth in 1919. But I was wrong about the rest. All a country has to

*Correspondence: Anthea Hyslop Email: anthea.hyslop@bigpond.com

Archives & Manuscripts © 2023 Anthea Hyslop. Published by Australian Society of Archivists. This is an Open Access article distributed under the terms of the Creative Commons Attribution-NonCommercial-NoDerivatives License (https://creativecommons.org/licenses/by-nc-nd/4.0/), which permits sharing the work provided it is properly cited. The work cannot be changed in any way or used commercially without permission from the journal.
Archives & Manuscripts 2023, 51(1): 10955 - http://dx.doi.org/10.37683/asa.v51.10955

47

do these days is to declare that no plane from this or that foreign clime will be allowed to land here. And then, when it is allowed, the passengers must undergo compulsory quarantine – in designated hotels, if nothing else be available. I was wrong, too, about the kind of disease that would be involved: *not* an influenza of any type, but instead a mysterious coronavirus, for which there was no known cure, let alone a vaccine. In this respect, the new pandemic was reflecting that of 1918–1919 even more closely than I'd expected. Their main differences appeared to be as follows: firstly, those people worst affected – this time the elderly and the vulnerable, rather than the young and fit; secondly, the much greater capacity of today's medical science to respond to a new virus – progress that owes much to the challenge of pneumonic influenza; and lastly, the mortality of each pandemic – far greater everywhere from 'Spanish flu' than from COVID-19: albeit, for Australia, in each instance mercifully less heavy than elsewhere.

For historians, then, I think the questions raised by COVID-19 in Australia will be similar to those posed by the pneumonic influenza pandemic. Where did it come from? How did it enter the community? How was it spread and controlled? How did governments respond, and with what measures? What happened, and why, if their schemes went awry? How did medical science approach the problem of a new and dangerous disease? How did the community react to the pandemic threat and to the constraints that its management imposed? What were the ordeal's longer-term consequences?

With COVID-19, as with pneumonic influenza, the dealings between federal and state governments are a central theme. In November 1918, the health ministers and senior health officials from around the country gathered in Melbourne, at that time the home of the federal government, to formulate a national plan for meeting the pandemic's onslaught. That conference was a single event, and the agreement that emerged soon fell apart over border closures, halted trains and other quarantine problems; but a century later, it furnished an example of sorts for 2020's National Cabinet. The November Agreement of 1918 and its gradual unravelling were well reported in the daily press, and the official record may be found at the National Archives: a veritable goldmine of formal reports, letters and innumerable telegrams between federal and state governments. I hope that 'cabinet confidentiality' will not have prevented 2020's 'remote' National Cabinet meetings from being recorded, both in video and in transcript, and that the related traffic of emails will survive as well as all those long-ago telegrams did. Both then and now, such records reveal much about the dynamics of federal-state relations under conditions of stress, and the extent of their respective emergency powers.

In 1918–1919, maritime quarantine was in the hands of the federal director of quarantine, Dr JHL (Howard) Cumpston, and careful records were kept of activities at the several coastal quarantine stations around the country. Yet in January 1919, after several months of impressive success, pneumonic influenza escaped into the community at Melbourne, the interim federal capital, and how it had done so could not then be established. That puzzle helped to delay both federal and Victorian health authorities in recognising it as the dread disease: a delay that allowed it not only to spread in Melbourne but also to travel by train to Sydney before any borders were closed. Today, the puzzle would have been swiftly solved by genomic analysis of viral samples, which might also have traced the symptomless carrier now surmised to have brought the 'flu' out of quarantine and into Melbourne. But in 1919, any knowledge of viruses was in its infancy, and influenza was regarded as a bacterial disease. I trust that the full story of 2020's quarantine failures, whether Sydney's *Ruby Princess* cruise ship saga or Melbourne's hotel quarantine breakdown, will be preserved for posterity in the records of the formal enquiries that followed.

On the other hand, I have no doubt that the role of medical science in this pandemic will be exhaustively recorded. It has been fascinating to observe modern medicine responding again,

Archives & Manuscripts 2023, 51(1): 10955 - http://dx.doi.org/10.37683/asa.v51.10955

as it did in 1918, to an unknown and highly infectious pandemic disease. Back then, with bacteriology the new field of achievement, medical scientists worked frantically to produce a bacterial vaccine. Here in Australia, the young Commonwealth Serum Laboratories quickly developed one, as did state pathology labs, and supplied several million doses in the space of 6 months to a remarkably receptive public. That bacterial vaccine could not waylay the virus, but it did appear to reduce the impact of secondary bacterial infections. Today's medical science response has been able to deploy the enormous benefits of a century's progress in virology. Likewise, with COVID-19, the medical and nursing professions have been able to draw on highly sophisticated technology and pharmaceutical research. By contrast, their counterparts in 1918–1919 could do little beyond treating influenza's symptoms and providing careful nursing, although both these things went far toward helping patients survive. Doctors tried hard to find effective cures, as may be seen in the pages of the *Medical Journal of Australia*; but amid the crisis most would have had scant time to spare for experiment.

The broader community's experience of a pandemic may emerge in various ways. That of 1918–1919 can be found in part in municipal records of relief distributed to families whose breadwinners had lost their employment or, worse, had died. It appears also in letters to newspapers of the time, or in private diaries and letters fortuitously preserved. Half a century would pass before scholars began soliciting survivors' recollections of pneumonic influenza. One of the first was Richard Collier, a British author and journalist, who in 1972 sought responses from around the world to incorporate in a book entitled *The Plague of the Spanish Lady* (1974). Among his correspondents were some 150 Australians who recorded for him their own memories or those of their families. Around 15 years later, New South Wales scholars conducting interviews with octogenarians for Australia's bicentenary unearthed further memories of the pandemic that followed the Great War. In both sources, these private recollections may have been faded a little by time, but they are unaffected – unexaggerated? – by any sense of their significance as part of a great world drama. With today's pandemic, personal experiences gathered now will have greater immediacy and will probably reflect their global context more strongly – if only because modern news media have conveyed that global context so clearly.

Indeed, many of our daily newspapers quickly began gathering experiences of lockdown, hardship and sickness, alongside family reminiscences of beloved older members lost to COVID-19. Press, radio, television and websites have together collected formidable amounts of information, analysis and detailed description of this pandemic. By contrast, in 1918–1919, newspapers were almost the only public medium, and photographic images from that pandemic were chiefly confined to illustrated weeklies like the *Sydney Mail*. Media records from today's pandemic, provided they continue to be accessible, will present for historians a research resource of almost overwhelming proportions.

A further burden for future researchers will be the extraordinary length of the current pandemic – 3 years so far, and with new viral variants still emerging. By contrast, Australians' encounter with the 'flu' pandemic's severe second and third waves lasted only half as long: from cases among our soldiers overseas, in August 1918, to a final isolated outbreak in Far North Queensland, in early 1920. For the Australian community itself, the pandemic experience endured for barely a year, from January 1919 in Melbourne to January 1920 on Thursday Island. Indeed, in most of the country, the 'flu' had faded out by late 1919. Today, the current pandemic appears to be declining slowly, and COVID-19 may well become, like influenza, an annual visitor of varying severity, for which we shall be reasonably well prepared.

The history of the 1918–1919 influenza pandemic is at one level a record of public dramas and private tragedies amid a great human crisis. Deeper down, it also reveals much about how society functioned in more normal times, throwing light on themes that might not seem to bear on the crisis but were nevertheless significant elements of ordinary life. I feel confident that our current pandemic will reveal to historians at least as much as its predecessor has done – about how, in all manner of ways, we were living our lives, before it turned them upside down.

A note on sources

For those parts of this article dealing with COVID-19, I have drawn on common knowledge, rather than specific sources. For those dealing with the influenza of 1918–1919, I have drawn on my own research, contained in the following articles:

'A Question of Identity: J.H.L. Cumpston and Spanish Influenza, 1918–1919', in D. Walker and M. Bennett (eds), *Intellect and Emotion: Perspectives on Australian History. Essays in Honour of Michael Roe,* Centre for Australian Studies, Deakin University and Centre for Tasmanian Historical Studies, University of Tasmania, Geelong, 1998, pp. 60–76 (see also *Australian Cultural History*, no. 16, 1997/98); 'Insidious Immigrant: Spanish Influenza and Border Quarantine in Australia, 1919', in S. Parry (ed.), *Migration to Mining: Medicine & Health in Australian History. Collected Papers of the Fifth Biennial Conference of the Australian Society of the History of Medicine*, Historical Society of the Northern Territory and Australian Society of the History of Medicine, Darwin, 1998, pp. 201–215; 'Old Ways, New Means: Fighting Spanish Influenza in Australia, 1918–1919', in L. Bryder and D.A. Dow (eds), *New Countries and Old Medicine: Proceedings of an International Conference on the History of Medicine and Health, Auckland, New Zealand, 1994*, Auckland Medical History Society, Auckland, 1995, pp. 54–60; 'Forewarned, Forearmed: Australia and the Spanish Influenza Pandemic, 1918–1919', in J. Lack (ed.), *1919: The Year Things Fell Apart?*, Australian Scholarly Publishing, Melbourne 2019, pp. 30–43; 'The Great Pandemic of 1918–1919: Pneumonic Influenza in Australia', *Victorian Historical Journal*, vol. 93, no 2, December 2022, pp. 333–348.

Notes on contributor

Anthea Hyslop is an independent historian living in Melbourne. From 1989 until retirement in 2009, she lectured in History at the Australian National University in Canberra. Before that, she taught at Adelaide and Melbourne Universities, and at La Trobe University where she gained her PhD. She specialises in Australian history and the history of medicine: in particular, Australia's experience of the influenza pandemic of 1918–1919.

Note

1. This paper is an extended version of a paper presented in December 2020 to the UNESCO Memory of the World Program's Symposium on Documenting COVID-19 in Australia. It has also appeared, among other papers dealing with Australia's experience of the COVID-19 pandemic, in *Health & History*, vol. 25, no. 1, 2023, the journal of the Australian and New Zealand Society of the History of Medicine.

REFLECTION ARTICLE

Documenting COVID-19 in Australia: An Interdisciplinary Perspective

Terhi Nurmikko-Fuller*

Centre for Social Research & Methods, Australian National University, Canberra, Australia

Abstract

Social media posts and unpublished student projects are just two examples of the digital content – a type of ephemeral popular culture – produced during the COVID-19 pandemic. Collecting this material would provide researchers and analysts with information that is complementary to other data used to report and capture the crisis, such as government policies and scientific documentation. But what are the long-term privacy implications of collecting this material? In this time of privacy paradoxes and the Data Economy, does the responsibility for the ethical use of this data fall onto the archivists and researchers?

Keywords: *Digital ephemera*; *Ethics*; *Privacy*; *Social media*.

In January of 2009 – some 15 years ago – three professors from the University of Southampton, UK (Halford, Pope, and Carr) uploaded a manifesto describing the World Wide Web (henceforth 'the Web') as an object worthy of study in its own right: a thing that was the result of a 'co-constitution of technology and society… with heterogeneous actors – human and [software]… with a focus on the significance of performativity, suggesting that the web is less a thing and more an unfolding, enacted practice, as people interact with HTTP to build 'the web' moment by moment'.[1] They called this research space *Web Science*. This 'deliberately multidisciplinary'[2] field has examined the ways in which the Web has, over the last 30 years, emerged as a global information repository. It is a hypermedia platform; a stage for the performance of the self;[3] it became the new town square[4]; and, *inter alia*, the spreader of deep fakes, alternative facts, and misinformation. To study the Web in this context is to recognise that technological developments are affected by social pressures and desires, but also that society too changes under the influence of technology. This article explores how digital content could be archived and (ab)used to document our collective experience of COVID-19.

A study by researchers at the Harvard Kennedy School of Government, published in December 2021, found that whilst many social media platforms claimed to explicitly prohibit

*Correspondence: Terhi Nurmikko-Fuller, Email: terhi.nurmikko-fuller@anu.edu.au

the sharing of COVID-19-related misinformation, only four (Facebook, Instagram, YouTube, and Twitter) had a COVID-19 misinformation policy. Platforms such as Twitch, Tumblr, Messenger, and WhatsApp were not found to have explicit policies that sought to limit or prevent the spreading of misinformation about COVID-19.[5] But how effective are these policies? As of 23 November 2022, Twitter was no longer enforcing the COVID-19 misleading information policy[6]; and a study by the Institute for Strategic Dialogue (who describe themselves as 'an independent, non-profit organisation dedicated to safeguarding human rights and reversing the rising tide of polarisation, extremism and disinformation worldwide') criticised Facebook for what they described as a 'failure to tackle COVID-19 disinformation'.[7] Suter, et al found that up to 25% of comments on YouTube videos contained misinformation, and that, perhaps unsurprisingly, 'fake comments receive more attention and attract more fake replies than factual comments'.[8] Instagram, owned by Facebook, adheres to the latter's strategies for 'reducing the spread of misinformation',[9] but do not appear to be trying to actively completely prevent it.

The onset of COVID-19 brought along with it a proliferation of academic research (at the time of writing, the term brings up 4,330,000 results on Google Scholar[10]; 2,327,342 hits on WorldCat[11]; ResearchGate returns 100 pages with 10 full papers per page[12]; Arxiv returns 6,886 results).[13] The Australian Data Archive ('a national service for the collection and preservation of digital research data' based at the Australian National University (ANU) in Canberra)[14] contains 25 datasets reporting on the views of Australians on a range of COVID-19-related issues, from mental health and economic stress[15] to volunteering and aged care,[16] to name just two examples. The Australian Federal Government provides access to 143 datasets via https://data.gov.au. Add to this the plethora of analysis by academics who have examined COVID-19 in Australia from a number of different perspectives, some more generic,[17] others focusing on specific aspects such as its effect on public perception of the unemployed,[18] the consumption of alcohol at the beginning of an era that became epitomised by social distancing and lockdowns,[19] or the impact of the pandemic on teachers and students at all levels.[20] With a cornucopia of scientific research data available, why focus on social media posts to document the COVID-19 experience, in Australia and globally?

It is crucial to remember that social media platforms enable the collection and recording of (at least some of) the socio-cultural ephemera of our times. The incidental data snippets that capture the mundane are an extremely valuable and important part of creating a comprehensive picture of life during the pandemic. It might seem trivial, but photos of meals published on Instagram tell us about how our diets have changed during lockdown; analysis of lengthy posts on Reddit can help highlight social phenomena ranging from common trends to topics as significant as detecting suicide ideation in individuals who are struggling with complicated grief.[21] We can question whether it is possible to digitally map the spread of previous pandemics so as to predict the spread of this one by modelling information with the option of reinterpreting the data by changing one of several known variables. Or, we could focus on the other types of information generated during lockdowns, such as behavioural data from online gaming: since data from video game strategies can be used to model real-world crime syndicate behaviour,[22] could we also use it to predict or understand socially detrimental behaviours (for example, the decision of individuals to break lockdown curfew)? All these are examples of research carried out by graduate students at the ANU. Unfortunately, to my knowledge many of their findings, completed in the context of their studies, remain unpublished.

There are other areas of investigation that we may not yet have had a chance to touch on. Could Twitter serve as the platform for recording the chorus of a million academics lamenting another lecture delivered to a wall of turned-off cameras? Perhaps not, given the acquisition of the platform by Elon Musk in 2022[23] and the subsequent exodus of many academics to

Archives & Manuscripts 2023, 51 (1): 10957 - http://dx.doi.org/10.37683/asa.v51.10957

Mastodon.[24] And what of those videos on TikTok, the ones that did not go viral? Can they tell us about modern society and its values? And what can platforms that are popular beyond the anglophone world such as Sina Weibo[25] or QQ[26] tell us about the pandemic as a global phenomenon?

There is an abundance of user-generated data online. Researchers are keen to collect and analyse it, but where should we draw the line in our effort to document the pandemic? Considerations of privacy and ethics quickly come into play. Should we seek to collect and keep records of bored teenagers in lockdown sexting each other on SnapChat? Would any user want their private messages from encrypted platforms like WhatsApp recorded for posterity? Or exchanges over private email? But how does collecting this material (and the study of it by researchers of the future) differ from the work of historians reading private correspondence in archives and libraries? After all, these snippets from social media capture the world we live in, including the social phenomena of COVID-19: there is more (perhaps something more intangible, more inherently human) to the representation of the lived experience during the pandemic than data about the structures of the virus or the patterns of the spread and contaminations. Can we argue that social media posts are in some ways an insight (even if a curated one, and in some ways unrealistic one) into a global shared experience?

We know about some of the effects of 'long COVID', but there will be other longer-term effects of the pandemic that will only manifest to future generations. Is it our responsibility to provide future scholars with as comprehensive picture as possible? To document these exceptional times as comprehensively as we can? Perhaps so, but not without careful consideration of the challenges of preserving privacy and of the ethical collection, use, storage, and access to the collected data. This may be particularly poignant given phenomena such as the Privacy Paradox,[27] which stipulates that, although many may be aware of the risks of sharing data on social media (and this includes sites for the Quantified Self, such as Strava),[28] few users take concrete steps towards preserving their privacy when it comes to sharing content online. Does the onus of privacy protection rest with the researcher since the users seem unwilling to take on that responsibility? The last two decades have shown us that the platforms themselves (which have invested interests as commercial entities seeking to make a profit in the Data Economy)[29] are unlikely to step up to the plate.

Capturing the intangible culture of any place or context is undoubtedly riddled by the need to explicitly remember that any one individual's lived experience varies immensely from from person to person and not just from country to country or from one socio-economic or ethnic group to another. But moving aside for a moment from the social science context of focusing on individual people, how can we utilise the capacity of memory institutions and the GLAM (galleries, libraries, archives, and museums) sector to help document and enable research into the COVID-19? But what can our collections and our engagements with those collections tell us about COVID-19?

The pandemic might have defined the first few years of the 2020s, but it did not occur in isolation (all puns intended!). For Australia, and in the Australian Capital Territory (ACT) in particular, the year 2020 commenced with a big bang. The area suffered immense fires: in fact, the *Washington Post* declared the 2019–2020 Australian bushfire season as 'historic' and went on to state that on a global scale, the environmental impact of the fires was greater than that of COVID-19 lockdowns.[30] The National Museum of Australia (NMA) describes the fires as 'the longest and most intense experienced in our history'.[31] Then, in January 2020, the ACT experienced one of the single most severe hailstorms ever recorded in the area.[32] Following these events of fire and ice, a public health emergency was declared in March of the same year.[33]

The NMA made an effort to archive these tumultuous times: they called for members of the public to come forward with their stories to record them as part of Momentous[34]; a group called 'Fridge Door Fire Stories'[35] was established on Facebook[36]; and not only displayed a molten phonebooth from Cobargo,[37] but enabled students of the ANU to capture the phonebooth as 3D digital object[38] as part of their studies.[39] Other unpublished student projects include an animated children's book (aimed at helping young readers understand the impact and experience of the bushfires), as well as future-gazing mapping of the potential spread of the COVID-19 based on the historical records documenting the spread of pandemics of the past (particularly the so-called 'Spanish Flu'). As with the student-led examinations into social media, most of these projects tackling the challenges of capturing the lived experience of COVID-19 within the sphere of digital cultural heritage remain unpublished. It is hard to imagine that in this context the ANU would be singular example – rather, there are undoubtedly thousands of student-led and nascent investigations from hundreds of higher education institutions across Australia – and the world – experiencing the same.

During COVID-19, the slogan 'We're all in this together' became the government marketing rallying call. Whether attempting to boost public morale, compensate for social distancing, or 'mask public security',[40] it captures the notion of a shared experience, and a common benefit to be reaped from collaboration and the aggregation of resources. The same attitude could also be applied to data: aggregation and blending for benefit and synergies that provide insights that are much greater than the sum of their parts. What we need to do is take deliberate steps to capture and explicitly articulate tacit knowledge and minority (by which I mean something other than the mainstream media or the most popular social media) views and experiences. Even with the utilization of deep learning, machine learning and artificial intelligence (AI) (the tools *du jour*), we must invest in a comprehensive collection and capture of data, but also the representation of the information that we pull from that data that is derived in thoughtful ways.

As I have argued recently,[41] large-scale computational systems can and have gone horribly wrong in the past – such as the disgraceful (to say the least) case of Google Photos insouciantly racist tagging of images[42] or AI being used to generate recruitment advertisements for CEO positions that were then automatically sent exclusively to middle-aged white men (i.e., those who represented the historical model of previously successful applicants).[43] We have also seen AI reproduce bias in when used in criminal convictions of people in the USA.[44] We know that whilst technology is neither inherently good nor bad, per se, it is also clearly not neutral[45] and neither is the data, nor is the act of data collection. These are all riddled political decisions ranging from research aims to funding body decisions and beyond. The thoughtful and careful design of clear underlying data structures that represent different but equally valid knowledge perspectives are an absolute necessity if we seek to combine disparate datasets that hold complementary information.

Doing so at a vast scale at unprecedented speed is something that is technologically possible today but it is not just a matter of doing it, we need to do it well. As with any application of technological tools to a complex human problem we need to be careful not to succumb to temptation and the traps of technological determinism or lull ourselves into the belief that just because something is technological it is neutral, objective, and benign.[46] For it is none of them. We must also resist the ever-present temptation of editing and structuring the data that we collect to fit databases that we already have. Computational technologies should play a central role in our deliberate attempt to combine datasets from different places to accurately and faithfully document the COVID-19 experience. What we need is a coordinated, collaborative, shared effort and, crucially, the necessary investment into research to make this happen.

Notes on contributor

Dr Terhi Nurmikko-Fuller is a Senior Research Fellow at the Centre for Social Research & Methods at the Australian National University. Terhi's research focuses on interdisciplinary experimentation into ways digital technologies and computational methods can be used to support and diversify research in the Humanities, Arts, and Social Sciences in general, and in relation to public culture, including Web Science, and the cultural heritage sector in particular. Terhi's publications centre on topics related to Linked Data, knowledge representation, and digital libraries, but cover a range of other topics from the role of gamification and informal online environments to 3D digital models in museums. Terhi is a CI on an Australian Research Council-funded project (*Nyingarn: a Platform for Primary Sources in Australian Indigenous Languages*, led by University of Melbourne); and a member of the Territory Records Advisory Council, Australian Capital Territory Government.

Notes

1. Available at https://www.researchgate.net/publication/43652198_A_Manifesto_for_Web_Science, accessed 03 May 2023.
2. A phrase quoted from Kieran O'Hara and Wendy Hall, Four internets: Data, Geopolitics, and the Governance of Cyberspace, Oxford University Press, 2021, p. 245.
3. Erving Goffman, The Presentation of Self in Everyday Life, University of Edinburgh, Social Sciences Research Centre, Edinburgh, 1956.
4. Katrina Grant, 'Performances of Power-The Site of Public Debate', in Shirley Leitch and Paul Pickering (eds.), Rethinking Social Media and Extremism, ANU Press, Canberra, 2022, pp. 143–158.
5. Available at https://misinforeview.hks.harvard.edu/article/research-note-examining-how-various-social-media-platforms-have-responded-to-covid-19-misinformation/, accessed 07 June 2023.
6. Available at https://transparency.twitter.com/en/reports/covid19.html#2021-jul-dec, accessed 07 June 2023.
7. Available at https://www.isdglobal.org/isd-publications/ill-advice-a-case-study-in-facebooks-failure-to-tackle-covid-19-disinformation/, accessed 07 June 2023.
8. Viktor Suter, Morteza Shahrezaye, and Miriam Meckel, 'COVID-19 Induced Misinformation on YouTube: An Analysis of User Commentary', Frontiers in Political Science, vol. 4, 2022, p. 849763.
9. Available at https://help.instagram.com/1735798276553028, accessed 07 June 2023.
10. Available at https://scholar.google.com.au/, accessed 07 June 2023.
11. Available at https://www.worldcat.org/, accessed 07 June 2023.
12. Available at https://www.researchgate.net/, accessed 07 June 2023.
13. Available at https://arxiv.org, accessed 07 June 2023.
14. Available at https://ada.edu.au/, accessed 07 June 2023.
15. Nicholas Biddle, 'ANU Poll 48 (October 2021): Mental Health and Economic Stress During COVID 19', doi: 10.26193/THF1VZ, ADA Dataverse, V1, 2021, available at https://dataverse.ada.edu.au/dataset.xhtml?persistentId=doi:10.26193/THF1VZ, accessed 07 June 2023.
16. Nicholas Biddle, 'ANU Poll 50 (April 2022): Volunteering, Aged Care, Policy Priorities and Experiences with COVID-19', doi: 10.26193/AXQPSE, ADA Dataverse, V1. 2022, available at https://dataverse.ada.edu.au/dataset.xhtml?persistentId=doi:10.26193/AXQPSE, accessed 07 June 2023.
17. Dominic O'Sullivan, Mubarak Rahamathulla, and Manohar Pawar, 'The Impact and Implications of COVID-19: An Australian Perspective', The International Journal of Community and Social Development, vol. 2, no. 2, 2020, pp. 134–151. See also Jane Shakespeare-Finch, Holly Bowen-Salter, Miranda Cashin, Amalia Badawi, Ruth Wells, Simon Rosenbaum and Zachary Steel, 'COVID-19: An Australian perspective', Journal of Loss and Trauma, vol. 25, no. 8, 2020, pp. 662–672.
18. Aino Suomi, Timothy P. Schofield, and Peter Butterworth, 'Unemployment, Employability and COVID19: How the Global Socioeconomic Shock Challenged Negative Perceptions toward the Less Fortunate in the Australian Context', Frontiers in Psychology, vol. 11, 2020, p. 594837.
19. Erica Neill, Denny Meyer, Wei Lin Toh, Tamsyn Elizabeth van Rheenen, Andrea Phillipou, Eric Josiah Tan, and Susan Lee Rossell, 'Alcohol Use in Australia during the Early Days of the COVID-19 Pandemic: Initial Results from the COLLATE Project', Psychiatry and Clinical Neurosciences, vol. 74, no. 10, 2020, pp. 542–549.

20. Rachael H. Dodd, Kevin Dadaczynski, Orkan Okan, Kirsten J. McCaffery, and Kristen Pickles, 'Psychological Wellbeing and Academic Experience of University Students in Australia during COVID-19', International Journal of Environmental Research and Public Health, vol. 18, no. 3, 2021, p. 866.

21. This refers to on-going work by Xinyuan Xu, building on her prior work on social media mourning: see for example Xinyuan Xu, Terhi Nurmikko-Fuller, and Bernardo Pereira Nunes, 'Tweets, Death and Rock'n'roll: Social Media Mourning on Twitter and Sina Weibo', in Proceedings of the 10th ACM Conference on Web Science, 2018, May, pp. 297–306.

22. Robert Fleet and Terhi Nurmikko-Fuller, 'The Potential for Serious Spaceships to Make a Serious Difference', in Proceedings of the 11th ACM Conference on Web Science, 2019, June, pp. 97–104.

23. Available at https://www.nytimes.com/2022/10/27/technology/elon-musk-twitter-deal-complete.html, accessed 08 June 2023.

24. Available at https://www.insidehighered.com/news/2022/12/01/academics-twitter-disperse-wake-musk-take-over#:~:text=Fiesler%20remains%20on%20Twitter%20but,much%20higher%20than%20on%20Twitter, accessed 08 June 2023.

25. Available at https://english.sina.com/weibo/, accessed 07 June 2023.

26. Available at https://im.qq.com/index/, accessed 07 June 2023.

27. Available at https://stories.uq.edu.au/business/2020/privacy-paradox-data/index.html#:~:text=However-er%2C%20only%20a%20small%20percentage,studied%20about%20two%20decades%20ago, accessed 07 June 2023.

28. Available at https://www.strava.com/, accessed 07 June 2023.

29. Available at https://www.technologyreview.com/2021/11/16/1040036/capitalizing-on-the-data-economy/, accessed 08 June 2023.

30. Available at https://www.washingtonpost.com/weather/2021/07/27/australian-bushfires-smoke-climate-covid/, accessed 07 June 2023.

31. Available at https://www.nma.gov.au/explore/features/momentous, accessed 07 June 2023.

32. Available at https://knowledge.aidr.org.au/resources/hailstorm-act-january-2020/#:~:text=One%20of%20the%20most%20severe,to%20the%20inner%20southern%20suburbs, accessed 07 June 2023.

33. Available at https://www.cmtedd.act.gov.au/open_government/inform/act_government_media_releases/rachel-stephen-smith-mla-media-releases/2020/public-health-emergency-declared-for-act, accessed 07 June 2023.

34. Available at https://www.nma.gov.au/explore/features/momentous, accessed 07 June 2023.

35. The significance of the fridge is explained in this article from Canberra Weekly: Available at https://canberraweekly.com.au/famous-firies-fridge-on-display/, accessed 07 June 2023.

36. Available at https://www.facebook.com/groups/fridgedoorfirestories/, accessed 07 June 2023.

37. Available at https://www.abc.net.au/news/2022-07-03/natural-disaster-cobargo-melted-phone-booth-canberra-museum/101196906, accessed 07 June 2023.

38. Available at https://sketchfab.com/3d-models/cobargo-phonebooth-2-e0b984f0253148e58328f0007b5f10ef, accessed 07 June 2023.

39. The courses as delivered in the previous years are described in Katrina Grant and Terhi Nurmikko-Fuller, 'Students as Collaborators: A Digital Humanities and GLAM Sector Collaboration to Produce New Web-Based Content Through Student Led Projects', in MuseWeb 2021, available at https://mw21.museweb.net/paper/students-as-innovators-a-digital-humanities-and-glam-sector-collaboration-to-produce-new-web-based-content-through-student-led-projects/index.html, accessed 07 June 2023.

40. Available at https://www.afr.com/politics/pandemic-slogans-mask-public-scrutiny-20210616-p581n6, accessed 07 June 2023.

41. Terhi Nurmikko-Fuller, Linked Open Data for Digital Humanities, Routledge, 2023.

42. Available at https://www.theverge.com/2018/1/12/16882408/google-racist-gorillas-photo-recognition-algorithm-ai, accessed 27 May 2022.

43. Available at https://www.independent.co.uk/life-style/gadgets-and-tech/news/google-s-algorithm-shows-prestigious-job-ads-men-not-women-10372166.html, accessed 25 February 2021.

44. Available at https://www.technologyreview.com/2019/01/21/137783/algorithms-criminal-justice-ai/, accessed 25 February 2021.

45. Melvin Kranzberg, 'Technology and History: "Kranzberg's Laws"', Technology and Culture, vol. 27, no. 3, 1986, pp. 544–560.

46. Terhi Nurmikko-Fuller and Paul Pickering, 'Crisis, what crisis?', in Shirley Leitch and Paul Pickering (eds.), Rethinking Social Media and Extremism, ANU Press, Canberra, 2022, pp. 159–178.

Archives & Manuscripts 2023, 51 (1): 10957 - http://dx.doi.org/10.37683/asa.v51.10957

www.ingramcontent.com/pod-product-compliance
Lightning Source LLC
Chambersburg PA
CBHW080402030426
42334CB00024B/2969